Patterned
FAST-BREAK
Basketball

J. Ted Carter

Parker Publishing Company, Inc.   West Nyack, N.Y.

PRINTED IN THE UNITED STATES OF AMERICA
ISBN—0-13-654079-1
BC

What Our Controlled Run-and-Gun Game Will Show You

The grand old game of basketball has made great changes in recent years. It has developed new style and flair that makes it at once a "fun" game. And yet there's a "frugality" of movement about it that would make an efficiency expert dance for joy. Three years ago we began to study this new style. The results of that study you see before you in this book.

We are excited by this brand of ball. Fans love it. Players love it and, to top all that, it's a winning brand of ball! We know it—we play it. We call it the "Run, Gun and Have Fun" game, yet it's a lot more than that. It combines the rough tough skills of the football player with the mobile abilities of the tough, slender, small athlete. It's a "body contact" game and yet it shows to best advantage the abilities of the super-athlete as no other game ever did. A team runs its patterns so fast that many sportsmen think they are completely free-lance. It is intended that they should think so. This style makes fans who have never seen a game before, suddenly adopt a team!

I've heard casual salesmen from as far away as several hundred miles praise our athletes, and brag to nearby customers after they've seen us for the first time, "You ought to see those boys. They can do everything with the ball but eat it."

And yet, we're not showboats. We do only what is absolutely necessary to put the ball through the hoop. We use our fanciest moves only when they are needed. We pass to get open, then we shoot the ball.

A critical sports writer once said about one of our ball-handlers, "He makes the most difficult play look easy." That's the greatest praise an athlete can ever have. A scout for a "Big Ten" club said, after watching another player one quarter, "He's got all the moves I was looking for."

This "new" game isn't easy to teach. It must be carefully studied. The coach must use "individual" psychology on each of his players. When he is successful in doing so, when he is successful in welding his team of athletes with great moves into one unit, he has created a thing of beauty and a joy to behold. His team is a symphony of fluid motion, grand opera of the gymnasium—ballet on the basketball court.

We haven't had many teams like that, but then we haven't been coaching this way all our lives.

Our own players forced us to "go back to school" to study the "new look" carefully, to take second thoughts, revise our philosophy—trade some of our old ideas about the game. That we have done, but we've kept a lot of our tried and true ideas, and every year we've added to those ideas. Our athletes keep us young trying to keep up with them. They're the best teachers we've ever had. So this book we dedicate to them: To the youngsters of all the years. They now combine the arts of the basketball ages with the enthusiasm of youth—if the coach lets them do it.

This is what we try to do: Simply speaking, we give them efficient, well-thought-out patterns that provide them certain advantages. We run them until their tongues are hanging out to get them in shape; then we let them play.

Here in this book are the patterns and the drills we use. We hope they will help you. We can't guarantee they'll work for you, though, as they do for us. We can't even guarantee that we'll use them ourselves tomorrow. The type of material, the abilities of the players, the type and style of opposition often dictate more than the coach the style of play to be used. We can guarantee only one thing: This study won't hurt you and you'll have the time of your life if you use it.

TED CARTER

Explanation of
Some Basketball Terms Used

Double Team Areas—In the foul lane where a pivot man can be double teamed from front and rear, yet the guard who drops off his man to double team is able to recover without allowing his man an open shot. Other safe areas are in or near each corner and near the center line where a ballhandler can be isolated.

Elbow Hook—Player with ball puts elbow in front of defense to keep him away from ball.

Free Lance—Allowing players to get open by using their own individual skills.

Freezing onto the Ball—Unable to pass at the opportune moment.

Full-Court Game—Playing on the full court, rather than dividing the court into a defensive and offensive half. Full-court plays and drills run from one base line to the other. This is the modern game. Just a few years ago teams yelled "slow it down," then they set up offensive patterns on the half court.

Get Him on Your Back (Defensive)—This means as soon as the ball is released for a shot at the basket, the defensive player-rebounders should block out by turning to face the basket, feet wide apart, arms out and back, "holding" their men behind them by feeling and fighting their opponents' pressure towards the basket.

Keeping Defense on Your Back—It is difficult for the men who play with their backs to the basket to know where the defensive player is unless he can feel him with his hands. He soon learns to reach back and locate his opposition; then he can hook him with a hand or a pivot step, and keep him behind his back for the good shot close to the basket.

Leap Frog Tactics—A defensive move along the sidelines. On a press situation, an offensive dribbler gets away from his man. The next defensive man up the court slows the dribbler down while playing both his own man and the dribbler. As soon as the passed pressing guard can catch up with the dribbler, he goes straight to his teammate's man (not the dribbler). Thus the defense switches or "leap frogs" because the back guard has good defensive position.

A note to remember: It is usually fatal to double team here against a good ballhandler. He'll eat you up, pass the ball to the open man for an easy layup.

Moving Screens—According to the rulebook this is illegal—we mean a "weaving" brand of ball whereby there is motion and a player who doesn't switch or fight across the screens in front of ballhandlers is left behind. If he switches then the the inside roll, whereby the offensive player hooks his man behind him is effective.

Penetrating Guard—An excellent ballhandler and dribbler who can take the ball within good shooting distance of the basket through the opposition's "outer line of defense." He can then score from the good-percentage shooting areas or pass off accurately to teammates for good shots.

Reverse Hooking Pivot—Offensive dribbler handles an overplaying guard by inviting him to go for the ball, then as he leans, reverse pivots hooking the defense behind him.

Rocker Dribble—A swaying motion of the dribbler's body, somewhat like rocking chair motion, whereby the dribbler gets his defensive man swaying with him; then, as the defense starts to sway backward to the rhythm, he suddenly explodes to go for the basket, leaving the defense going the other way.

Tear Ball out of Pile-Up—The ball comes down in a pile-up; everybody's grabbing at it. The player who brought it down should keep both hands on it, keep it against his stomach, lean towards the area he wants to go out, and "tear" the ball out in front of him by using his body to knock any hands out of the way. He should "throw" the ball out of the back by dribbling out in front of him. His momentum will take him "through" the ball and out into the open, leaving the pack behind and opening up 2-on-1 or 3-on-2 opportunities.

Timing—Ability to cut when the ball is in passing position or ability to pass at just the right moment.

Table of Contents

Chapter 13—continued

Patterned Fast-Break Basketball

1

Advantages of the Patterned Fast-Break Attack

We play a style of ball we call the "Run, Gun and Have Fun" game. We believe a player must enjoy the game to be good at it, so we direct all our drills and patterns toward enjoyment and efficiency. When our drills become boring to the players, we change them or we go home. We use no exercises that are distasteful. Necessary exercises can be better experienced in teaching situations that the players can enjoy—competitive situations. We use no drills such as rope skipping, weight lifting, or cross-country running.

There are too many things an athlete can do on the court with the basketball to waste time with vaguely-related drills. We have rebounding machines available, but we've found drills using the board and the hoop to be more effective.

If an athlete wishes to play around in the off season with the form of exercise his classmates are using, we allow him to do so, but we don't especially encourage him.

Use of Drills

All our drills are related to developing "full court" skills in the game. We desire a player to be agile and mobile, but we don't especially want him hostile. We just want him tough and able to bristle up, rise to whatever challenge may be thrown at him. We want him to enjoy contact and to glory in tough boardwork, defensive play and going for the loose balls. We want him to do all those things with a smile of enjoyment on his lips. We teach him to stand tall and walk proud. When he does so, we know we've got ourself a real ballplayer who has confidence enough in himself not to quit when the going is tough. That's the kind that wins titles! We train for the "tough" games and let the easy ones take care of themselves. We usually win those without extra training, providing we're basically sound and psychologically level-headed.

For every drill we use, we want a challenge thrown at the player. We want pressure put on him. Relaxed, YMCA-style ball is fine for physical education, but it doesn't suffice for the competitive athlete.

When we put all our training drills together to develop our style of play, we want no free-lance ball except at given times and under certain conditions. Always we move quickly and with purpose—within certain set lanes. We do it with the idea of gaining certain advantages. Only when we get those advantages do we fire away; and even then we "make haste" to recover any missed shots. We never give the ball up cheaply. We take only the percentage shots, close, or with one foot on the foul circle, and always with a good rebound angle.

We've found that in this style of ball our greatest troubles come from players who at first can't "free lance" in our style of ball. They get mixed up when we tell them to take into consideration there are nine other players on the floor. They feel a bit "stifled," won't take the shots when they are open. They sometimes "freeze onto the ball," fail to turn it loose at the right moments. This type of player seems always to want to "get a bit closer." That isn't our style at all. We study our players and desire them to shoot freely from the area where most their talent is. They can "strut their stuff"—but only where their talent lies and within the limits set by the patterns. We tell the whole squad what each player is supposed to do and they soon learn to expect *exactly that* out of those players. They then get used to each other much quicker.

Our players get exasperated at the athlete who has no "timing," who passes at the wrong time, gets to his position before the ballhandler is in position. Our greatest problems are curing the player of those untimely moves.

Usually we uncover not more than three or four players on our squad who have those timely moves and the ability to turn the ball loose at exactly the right moment. Those players seem to have hands and feet that think separately and yet together. We choose these for our varsity.

Team Leaders

Sports writers often call our team leaders "unselfish" ballplayers. That isn't really exactly the word to use. They're just "team" players who glory in making the hard play, who zip the ball around to get a man open because that is what they want to do. We've seen them make three or four terrific passes with proper moves toward the basket, have the fans clapping their hands, beating their thighs, raising clinched fists in appreciation to the accompaniment of thunderous approval. Even the defensive players admire such movements, and often nod or shake their heads in disbelief.

Frankly, we think coaches who force their players into a slow tempo of ball are wrong. Watching a team play basically defensive ball, gain ball possession, give the ball off to some little guard who stands with out-stretched hands waiting, then walking down the court while the big men trot into proper positions is actually boring. As one coach put it, "It's about as interesting as watching paint dry."

The athlete has no chance to show his real abilities.

Fast-break pattern ball enables the athlete to operate smoothly and without haste at top speed. His feet streak, yet his arms and hands seemingly operating independently in a deliberate manner. In the midst of all the action, you see the calm, perfectly balanced shots and passes like frozen motion. We name that athlete who can perform in such a manner "a super athlete" or "a ballplayer's ballplayer." Our fast-break ball lets them show their wares to the fan's approving cheers and yet it is no helter-skelter style. It's all done to distinct patterns with everybody knowing what everybody else is about to do. Even the defense knows it; but if our timing is perfect, there's little he can do about it.

2

Five Keys to the Patterned Fast-Break Style

Patterned fast-break ball is controlled ball played at top speed. It's a difficult game to play. It takes a special type of player. This athlete must be well-balanced in his moves and he must be good on defense. He must have quick hands. He must be an excellent rebounder. He must be calm and deliberate and he must be capable of explosive movements when the proper time comes. Over and above all, he must be well grounded in our patterned type of play so that he and his teammates know by heart exactly what is going to happen before it happens. They react together and finally they must contain themselves when it becomes obvious that their quick reactions have not secured the desired results. Our team, then, should be a patient team, running fixed patterns to get open for the good percentage shot.

In order to find proper players to fit our patterned fast-break style of play, we drill our squad, selecting our team carefully with the five keys to our fast break in mind—we teach more than passing, shooting, dribbling, team play and level-headed action. Our "keys" must be executed in certain special ways.

Passing the Ball

We don't teach the "push pass," "the bowling pass," "the hook pass" and other conventional styles. When we find a player who is weak in any of those, we tell him to improve the pass on his own. He usually does that. What we do teach is to pass the ball from where you catch it, if quick passing is needed. For that, the player needs strong wrist action. He "moves the ball on" from where he receives it without telegraphing his punch. The fake, if a fake is needed, is made from there, too. It takes a lot of stamina and strength to move the ball in this fashion. The soles of the passer's shoes must usually be firm against the floor and "scraping on it." The power of the pass comes all the way from his toes, which are pressing hard against the floor for traction. A player who is constantly in the air can't make such quick moves. He must be crouched down, muscles contracted. Then his passes have some zing and sting in them. He doesn't worry what he looks like. He just gets the ball to where its supposed to be with the least wasted motion.

One split second's hesitation, a fumbled ball, or a drawback for a telegraphed pass will ruin our fast break. We don't worry about opponents "playing our passes." We have options on impromptu presses that take care of overplays. We fall automatically into them whenever an overplay takes place. The ball is passed to the most advantageous position where it is rapidly moved into scoring position. We always tell our players that on the tail end of the fast break, go to the foul circle with the ball for a jump shot. We emphasize *they should go for the shot*. That takes the passing worry off their mind. Then, when they get up in the air, they may find someone open for a layup. They drop the ball into his hands.

On half-court pattern play, especially on out-of-bounds plays, we pass the ball in from over the head. These plays are "move on" fingertip plays. The ball moves from one player to the other, over and in front of the head. Passes are made from where the ball is caught in those positions with no "drawbacks." The offensive player lines himself up on the defense so he has a clear shot at pivot and post men who are to receive the ball. If a post or pivot is overplayed, an option is given for the player to take. If everyone is covered, we have an option for that, too. The overplayed players fake, reverse themselves, grab a lane cutting for the basket. The ballhandler dribbles himself open into the area of the foul circle and shoots or hits one of the cutters. The better the defensive press on these plays, the better they work, providing our players don't chicken by holding onto the ball a second or so too long.

We use a baseball type pass on all long passes. We prepare before we receive the ball, to pass it on. We catch the ball in a position to move it without drawing back or telegraphing. We start our movement for a "spot" pass on the floor. The cutter must get there. If the pass is overplayed, the passer hits the ball into the palm of his left hand and starts a quick dribble down the court. One dribble usually gives the side cutter time to clear himself. Then the passer hits him for a driving layup. We don't practice "leading the man" on long passes. We tell our players to "hit the man." Hit him "where his hands are"—up or down, depending on how he's running.

All close passes, we teach as underhand passes. We want the ball to move quickly, but we don't want heavy, hard-to-handle passes. Heavy passes make the receiver tighten up his wrists and fingers, often making him miss the crip shot before he can relax his forearms again. The receivers must always keep their hands up and at the waist, with elbows bent and "locked." This ability to "lock" the elbows, so the hands are always in front of the body, is an art few players master. If the receiver doesn't work on this, then a "quick" passer will often hit him in the stomach with the ball—sometimes in the face. A few bloody noses will teach the big pivot men to get their hands up.

Against a zone press, we teach quick "yo-yo" passes between the three fast-break lanes (middle to side, back to middle) as defensive men attempt to guard two men. And we go quickly for the boards. There should be no long, angle passes. We've found that two, maybe three passes are all that are necessary for a team to be shooting crip shots on a pressing defense.

Shooting

We select our shooters with five things in mind: (1) the position from which he releases the ball when guarded closly by an opponent; (2) closeness of his hands to the basket when he releases the ball; (3) the accuracy of his shots; (4) his rebounding ability and natural rebounding position; (5) his desire to get into the fight under the basket.

If a shooter "presses" when he is closely guarded, then he is apt to throw the ball away on his shots. We watch how he gets the ball up, where he releases the ball from, and where his eyes are when he releases it. This is something that can't be taught. It comes from long hours of playing alley ball against rough competition during the formative years. Unorthodox shots are often developed that way; if the player hits constantly, we don't try to change him. Once we attempted to teach only jump shots going to the boards; now we let the shooters alone, even on a fall-away shot and shots running from the basket. The player must be studied as to his "total" offensive strength. He may be compensating for "fade away" tactics through another effective action.

Once, we even worried about how a player held his hand when releasing the ball on a crip shot. We even tried to teach that the palm must face the board. Other years we taught a layup with the ball leaving the fingertips, hand pointing at the basket, palms up. Now we don't bother with that at all. Most players develop their own distinct styles. We leave them alone, tell them to get into position for rebounds in case of misses, and develop a player as a trailer just to be certain.

We like to have our players start their shots from safe positions where they won't get the ball batted or stolen before they get in the release position. We tell them that, after they get the ball up, they should go as close to the basket as they can above everybody's head to the basket before the release. Often they go up and change the position of the ball in mid-air to get closer on release.

We learned in this past year a lot from the pros on crip shots. The teams we're playing now often use goal-tending big men who can block shots or pin them to the boards before they start their downward flights. That's all perfectly legal. We teach our players to do as the pros did against the great Bill Russell— carry the ball all the way to the hoop, release the ball against the board in the little triangle formed by the hoop and the surface of the back board. The only way that shot can be blocked is by fouling the shooter or illegally goal tending.

Our shooters must always be ready for the second and third shots on every attempt. More points are scored on rebounds than any other way. We look for those "garbage" rebounders when we form our team. We can use one of them—not more—to give us power under the boards. The ball seems to fall into those players' hands. They may not be good pivots—they just get rebounds on each end of the court.

We like our shooters to be "buzz saws"—perpetual motion! They must be constantly hawking the ball on offense as well as defense. They must go after the rebounds and loose balls as if life depends on it. They must dive all over the floor to get it.

We especially detest the shooter who hangs around until somebody gets him in a shooting position and hands him the ball. Then, after practice, he can always tell you how many points he scored. We like players who get their own shots, the rebounds and loose balls, too. Anybody can shoot—if someone hands the ball to him.

Dribbling

We dribble only to go somewhere and then only after we see we can't shoot or pass the ball. Our "ABC's of Basketball" are: A—Shoot, B—Pass, C—Dribble, in that order.

Our dribble, when close to the basket, is almost touching the ball to the floor with both hands "around" the ball all the time, fingers spread to protect it. The body is spread in a spider fashion to prevent the defense from coming around to steal it. The ball is flipped against the floor, the player doing little more than touching it, but with both hands covering the release and return. This must be done quickly so the pivot may take the necessary steps to get up to the boards before a double team, where an outside man drops off and the pivot is sandwiched. The dribble must be quick to prevent this. Sometimes when the defense is extra tough, the player may even dribble between his legs to get the ball into shooting position. Our motion on such a dribble in the congested pivot area is sort of crab-like, with the ball dribbled in the triangle area protected by the legs and thighs; sometimes the player even backs in. One coach calls this the "saddle."

The dribbler must make his move quickly, or he must get rid of the ball by passing. From the foul circle on, we emphasize only *one*, or at most, two dribbles are necessary—and never a dribble when a step will do.

For bringing the ball up the court by dribble, we prefer a high, hard, pumping action which keeps the ball pushing up into the palm of the hand, sometimes as high as in front of the dribbler's face. The head should always be held erect so that the whole court can be seen and pass opportunities taken advantage of. That's when we make our "secondary" fast break—from about the $3/4$ court line. As the dribbler crosses the center line, he begins to assume a more protective attitude toward the ball. As the defense approaches, he may "get his man on his back" when the defense becomes vulnerable to a "rocker" motion or a "reverse hooking pivot." We teach both those tactics as ways for the individual to get by the defense, along with screens and cuts off the pivots.

Teamwork

Basketball is a game of teamwork, but rarely on any one set play do more than two or three players get a piece of the action. The best "team play" usually takes place between a pair of forwards, a couple of good ballhandling guards, or a guard and a pivot man "feeder" who "like to play with each other." We've always found such combinations on teams with winning records. The team clicks best when those players are together. An injury to one of them often ruins a fine, winning streak.

All our patterns are built around the abilities of players who like to team up with each other. We watch for those combinations in every practice and in free-lance summertime games or alley play. We've seen young athletes start playing together in the grades, continue through the high school years, and enter championship play because they knew each other. We've seen potential champions broken up by coaches who did not understand this natural trait. Better players sometimes never become as successful as two or three not-so-talented youngsters who enjoy "team up."

Small high schools often develop winning teams every three years through this characteristic. The team wins everything one year, then the coach "starts all over with sophomores." (He excuses his loss in that statement.) As juniors, they begin to win again. As seniors they are usually of championship calibre. "Playing together" and naturally "teaming up" is the answer, so we work hard at finding players who team up on our own squads. We usually substitute two or three players together for that reason. We have pairs of guards and threesomes on the front line who know each other's characteristics. A selfish player who looks only for a shot—who hogs the ball—is actually rather useless to a coach who is trying to develop a winning spirit.

After we find our players with natural tendencies toward teamwork, we teach them to team up in twos or threes according to the defense and according to the immediate circumstance. This is a natural thing you watch for in your players—those who enjoy playing with each other and respect each other. The teaming up is done quickly before the defense can get help from other players.

The ball is moved quickly to take advantage of vulnerabilities and to disturb the thinking of the defensive player. An attempt is made to gain a psychological advantage by making the defense look foolish, so we pass quickly whenever the opportunity arises. Fans love this. The next time down, the defense may not even try to defend.

When the defense is equal to the offense, we key our remaining players to hurry into the play as trailers. One man arriving late may be the one to get the basket—a crip at that!

We use the long pass at any time a player is open. Easy baskets sometimes demoralize opposition.

In practice we never throw the ball to a "snowbird"—a player who is caught in the forecourt on a turnover of the ball, who constantly refuses to "put out" on defense. When that happens more than once, we stop practice, expose the player, make him run windsprints or substitute for him. Players must respect each other completely to have good team morale. If they do, then they never turn the ball loose with inward hesitation.

The squad knows players who "dog it." They know that the coach knows it, too.

"Level-Headed" Attitude

A good player must "see" the whole court, want to score points, and not care to whom they are credited.

No player can lose his temper and remain a good ballplayer. Any athlete who bristles at an opponent needlessly should be taken out of the ballgame immediately. If he gets mad at himself and slams the ball around, he should also be removed. No one can play good ball with "anger adrenalin" in his veins. Keys to success are players who want to win so badly they haven't time to worry about the opposition personally. They're too busy thinking about setting up teammates, scoring points and playing defense. That's the mark of champions.

No player should be allowed to openly question an official's decision or even make motions of disgust or question at his teammates or to the coach on the bench. Such moves only serve to upset the rest of the players. The player should be trained to shoot his hand up quickly when a foul is called on him, as high and as straight as he can, then he should grin and wink at the official in an indulgent manner. He can gently shake his head, if he wishes, as the official looks at him. Then he takes his proper place and gets ready for the next move. If he's pleasant, the official may make up a missed decision in his favor later—that is, if he likes the player. That's only natural.

We've had athletes get knocked to the floor or tumble with a defensive player, get up and try to fight. We've had to remove them from the game temporarily losing them because of anger. We've had others pat an angry opponent on the fanny, grin at him and make him look foolish moments later on a defensive move or an attempt at the basket. The level-headed ones are the champions. The angry ones are plugs. We've never seen the angry ones, who bristle needlessly, win a championship. And on top of that, we've never seen an athlete who loses his temper play on a championship team in college.

These attitudes never change in an athlete from the grade school level into high schoool and on through college. A coach wastes time with the brawler. The level-headed ones with fiery competitive spirit win for you. We look for our brawlers and get rid of them. We treasure our level-headed ones. We don't have time to fool around with grumbling growlers.

3

Nine Guidelines for Selecting Patterned Fast-Break Personnel

When we look at our squad, we look first at four things: (1) the experience of the team, including perhaps most important- ly, the experience of the key ballhandlers; (2) the size and agility of the largest man; (3) the ability of the best ballhandler; (4) and, with no big man available, the over-all size of the best seven players on the squad.

This gives us an idea about our style of play for the year, often including the patterns for the season.

If we have a big man to rebound under both boards, then we can use smaller, more mobile players for the rest of the team. Of course we do not prefer small men to large mobile ones, but we've found that the players who are the best ballhandlers in junior high schools are little men. Most junior high coaches let those small players do all the ballhandling for their team. As a result, the big men come to us sadly deficient in ballhandling ability. They've "walked" down the court to "set up" under the boards; therefore, until we've trained good, big men for the backcourt, we go with the smaller men who already have the experience.

We are very careful, however, to take into consideration the outside shooting abilities of the little men. We can use one or two very small athletes, providing we have a towering center available, and providing the little men have extra speed, superior ballhandling ability and deadly shots from around the foul circle area. We never use a little man just for ballhandling ability alone. If he can't shoot from outside, then using him against big, powerful teams becomes too problematic to worry about. If he can't fast break, then he gives us problems on the pressing defenses. If he can't shoot from outside, then he's no use to us at all. Assuming that opposing coaches have at least average intelligence, and that they will discover the weaknesses of players after the first time around the league, in late-season games and for the playoffs, we'll see nothing but sagging defenses that zone and double-team under the boards. That gives far too much advantage to the defense for a little man to be profitable.

Anyone can stand outside and be a point man, swing the ball from side to side. The larger he is, the better. We must not waste strength and rebound ability if we do not have deadly accuracy from outside to compensate for it. Good teams in state tourneys always take advantage of such situations. Most teams who use non-scoring little men never make the tourneys. Crip shooting ability isn't enough.

If we have two big men, then we use three, speedy forwards who can hit from middle distances accurately. Two big rebounders can play close enough to the baskets on switching defenses to clear both boards almost constantly. They can also garner most of the rebounds on offense. Frankly, this is the type of team we work toward. We like a third, powerful man, but he must also be agile enough to be a ballhandler along with his rebounding power under the boards. It is better if he is a deadly shot from the corner. That balances our attack perfectly.

If we have three big men, with ballhandlers who aren't too

good, then we'll play a bit slower and a bit wider on the half court. It may be in this situation that we have to work harder for the good shot, use more screens and picks. We'll form a rebound triangle out of the big men on defense, shove our little ballhandlers further out front on full court set-ups, have them pressing the opposition's ballhandlers and almost "snow birding" on offense. The two must be perfectly matched for team play. They'll key off each other. On set patterns we'll use a jump shot-rebound game with little man working the ball in for crip shots.

If we have no big men, then we'll select all our ballplayers of medium stature. We can't gamble with little men in such a situation. We have to select five players who are well-balanced in all aspects of the game. They can have no individual weaknesses we would have to compensate for. Each player will have to carry an equal share of the load, both offense and defense.

For the ideal team, we pick our men by the following positions and for the following characteristics:

Corner Man

Ideally this player should be a corner shooter who hits well from outside, scores 12-16 points a game from that position, gets the rebound positions well, dribbles adequately, is able to feed the pivots well. He should be of good stature—the taller the better. He should be quick, have good hands, pass well, move out quickly to handle the ball whenever necessary. He should be the "third guard" on the team, plus the "third forward." He plays half inside and half outside. He should be able to grab one of the lanes on the fast break. Of vital importance, however, is this man's ability to understand that he must not play too deeply in the corner. When this happens, he sometimes becomes little more than a spectator watching while the opposition fast breaks the other way before he can come anywhere near getting back on defense. To keep this from happening, we line our corner men up about half-way between the end line and the foul line extended. We stress the defensive responsibility of this man when the guards are driving for the basket.

Pivot

This player doesn't have to be extra tall. In fact, an athlete from 6′ 4″ to 6′ 6″ is probably better in this position than a 7-footer who would get blocked away from the basket. Our pivot plays around the foul circle, cuts for the boards, and sometimes takes the low post position for hooks and jump shots. Mainly, however, he plays near the offensive foul shooting circle. He should have an accurate turning jump shot, and he should be able to drive right or left from the key hole. He should be able to hook well either right or left, be able to key the fast break, and dribble well. He should be a superb rebounder on both ends of the court and he should have the best, surest hands of any player on the floor. He must have that certain ability of good pivot men—to play with his back to the boards, handle the ball with defensive men all around him, and not lose the ball. At times he should be the high scorer—as much as 25-30 points a game.

Pivot-Forward

This should be the largest, toughest player. One nationally rated college coach called this player "the animal," and another outstanding mentor who has fielded national champions says he can have "two left feet" and still do the job. This player should be indestructable like a good college or pro football tackle. He should love the tough going under the boards. He doesn't have to be able to dribble too well, but he must be one of those "garbage" players who seems to be in the right place at the right time. He sets up the fast break off the defensive boards with his outlet passes. He often stays back, plays defense for his more mobile teammates on sudden slashes at the basket. This man should be able to get 12-15 points a game, mostly on rebounds. Nobody pushes him around, so usually he is assigned the opponent's best front-line man on defense.

Primary Ballhandler

This position should be filled by the key player around whom the team is to be built. He should be fast, quick and talented. He should be a good shot from outside, a fine dribbler, and a good driver who makes the crip shots and makes the good pass close to the basket. He should play $3/4$ offense to $1/4$ defense, but he must also have quick hands for steals on opponents' dribbles and against pivot men on defense. Our fast break often begins in this way. Above all, he should be able to penetrate the opponents' defenses.

He is our key man in tournaments when play has to be close to the vest, with few chances taken. He must be the team leader who draws the rest of the players along with him. This player must be the scoring leader, or near the top in statistics constantly. He should be the lead man on the fast break. We like for this player to be the "important" type rather than a "cool" leader. Basketball has become a game of "go and go." There's no time to play around with the ball, dribbling here and there. Players are so good now that they can usually get open for good shots with only a few moves. We like for them to take those shots without wasting time—then fight it out for the rebounds. On his good nights, with ordinary defenses, this man should score in the high 20s and 30s.

Secondary Ballhandler

This man should be the best outside shot on the team. He should play $3/4$ defense, $1/4$ offense. He should be able to stop or slow down the two-on-one fast break. He is the man you can depend on to "stay back" on offense to stop easy slashes at the basket. He should rarely drive for the basket, except when left wide open. He should score most of his points on jump shots from the outer half of the foul circle. Every now and then he can make a sudden slash at the basket, but he must quickly return to the back court. He should score 12-15 points a game from directly in front of the back board.

First Front-Line Substitute

This should be a "pivot man" who is tall, heavy and able to go briefly at top speed. He will be used only a short time to rest the front line men, and he should be able to play any of the three front positions. He shouldn't shoot too much, but he should be better than ordinary on rebounds and tipping the ball back in the hoop. He should be good at setting his teammates up, a leader in assists. He should be especially good on defense. The idea here is to rest key players and not hurt the team meanwhile. He should play a different style of ball from the regular starting forwards—"change of pace" makes him effective.

First Back-Line Substitute

This should be the third best ballhandler. Again, this man should be primarily a ballhandler and defensive player. It wouldn't hurt anything if he, too, were a "change of pace" type of player, in order to break the monotony of pattern and style of play of the game. It is better if he is quick and fast straightaway. A sudden substitution of a good man like this can sometimes upset the best teams, gain those few points that often change the whole tempo of the game, make the opposition play catch-up all night.

Utility Man

This player is the substitute called on when everybody fouls out. He may have to go in as forward or guard. He is capable of playing any position. This must be a smart player, even though he isn't the most talented. He is the fill-in player who sits on the bench, waits for his opportunity to come, is satisfied to do just that. We don't like to depend on a senior here. He isn't content to substitute; he doesn't have another year to look forward to.

The best utility man is a junior who probably won't match up in his final season. He's just below the first string in talent, but he's working hard to be better. He's a "thinking man" who knows what he's supposed to do in every position.

A Second Five

This should be almost a carbon copy of the first team, with the exception that these players should all be sophomores and juniors. Any senior on this team will hurt the morale, unless he understands his position and is willing to play second fiddle to the varsity with little chance of a starting role. Usually, this will be the group depended on to be the varsity next year, sprinkled with the seasoned veterans. This team should not try to play as fast as the first string. Rather, they should walk up and down the court, holding onto the ball a bit longer, working hard for good shots. The idea is that they learn to walk before they learn to run. This is also the group the varsity scrimmages against. If they try to run with their more seasoned brothers, they'll get clobbered and they'll lose their pride in ability.

Only the most exceptional sophomores should be carried on this varsity squad. A player who is too good for the "B" team or the junior varsity should be carried, however. We've found that the good ones in our area are targets of the recruitment processes of county high schools, private and parochial schools. You might lose him if you keep him down another year.

We've had only a few sophomores ever make our starting five, however. In those years, our teams didn't have the most brilliant records. Sophomores are rarely winners.

Our total squad consists of thirteen players. Fewer than this causes troubles on drills; more than this and everybody gets into everybody else's way.

No squad should ever be planned without keeping next year's team in mind. A "back up" man should be trained for every position. This should not be left up to the "B" team or junior varsity. The coach should personally train his own players and they should be getting used to him. Even junior varsity and

"B" teamers rarely make the varsity without going through a long, mixed-up training period where it seems they can do no right. That usually happens to them just before everything falls in place and they suddenly find themselves playing varsity-calibre ball.

The first requirement for these future stars is *desire* and a *fighting heart*. Other than that, considering they are average prospects, they'll absorb enough from the drills you run, the scrimmages and the few moments of substitution to be ready when next year comes.

The ideal team for winning year after year is the team that never graduates more than two or three players. At least two varsity returnees are needed to keep the record consistent. If as many as four starters graduate, then the 6th, 7th and 8th men should be juniors, plus all the second team.

4

Three Ways to Control the Game Tempo Through the Patterned Fast-Break System

Most good teams use a certain rhythm in their play. They try to make the opposition play their brand of ball. Sometimes it's a slow-down brand; sometimes it's race-horse ball. They play especially well when they find a team that attempts to match them.

We try to make our opposition play our style of ball, by several methods: (1) We hurry the ball down the court at all times in order to keep their defense alert. We don't want them to get their defense set or catch their breath on us. (2) Now and then we harry and harrass their ballhandlers. We want them to worry about just getting the ball across the center line, forget about feeding key men, but we don't take foolish gambles. We crouch and glide along in front of our defensive men ready to jump at them everytime they make a careless turn or edge into "double-team areas." We are often able to isolate the ballhandler; then we quickly throw on a press. (3) We use a pressing-switching-charging half court defense that sometimes looks like a zone press but actually is man-to-man; this enables us to fast break more efficiently. In fact, the key to our offense is our solid defense. The only time we free-lance on the full court is when we make interceptions or steals off the press.

Getting the Ball Down Court

In hurrying the ball down court, we like to use two or three passes. We try not to have one man dribble too much. We've found that the court is too long for players to dribble all the way, then have strength enough left to make proper moves on the drive for the bucket against good competition. Also, we do not like to spend our strength needlessly in the back court, so we try to hit a man at mid-court as soon as possible, let him penetrate a side or the middle while he is fresh and wanting to do something with it.

We make our little man get down court fast, then come back for the ball if necessary. Our big men can usually start a fast break with a dribble or so, then feed off to one of the ballhandlers cutting for a lane.

We actually turn our little men loose immediately after our opponent shoots. He leads our fast break. Our rule for this is: If your man takes a shot from outside, get him on your back for the block-out, then immediately cut down court to whichever side the pass-out is supposed to come. If the cutter is open, our rebounder hits him. If he is not, the rebounder starts his pass, *slaps the ball into his non-passing hand,* begins his dribble down court, then passes when open.

We like to hold our quick passes to the defensive end of the court and near the middle line. The approach to the basket should be by dribble to the jump shot area—but the ball should be moved by pass, not dribble. If we have the advantage near the foul circle, then the penetration should be attempted at once. We do not shoot from outside except when our rebounder is in position. If we have to wait for them, then we set up our half court patterns.

Harrassing the Opponent

If a team shows a readiness to shoot given reasonable opportunity, then we use a pressure man-for-man defense with everybody switching and charging on every crossover. We slow the cutters down for at least three steps to break their timing and we stay in position and ready for our fast break. If the opposition is prone to take long shots or drive in on a clogged-up basket area, then we sometimes use a zone on them. Players with quick hands can steal on the close-in drives through double-teams and, after a few successful far-outside shots, a team usually misses enough to give us a better percentage on our quick breaks from the zone. We'll match them basket for basket.

However, if a team plays pattern ball or a slow-down type that walks the ball down the court, then we attempt to change their natural style of ball by using a full-court defense. Our basic defense for this situation is a soft man-for-man that worries the ballhandler coming down the court, meets him tougher at the center line, and pulls his big men out of their favorite positions. This is not a full court press. It is merely playing your man all over the court, being ready for mistakes but putting the real pressure on him only when he is in a dangerous scoring position.

We use the press only in emergencies. We feel that it is an "ultimate" weapon; that when it is used, there is nothing left to fall back on. We sometimes throw the press on for a few moments of surprise action to change the tempo of the game, but it is not our basic defense. A full-court press team that has its press broken, sometimes becomes complete demoralized. Our man-to-man press begins with the throw in. We place a big man in front of the player who passes the ball in. We attempt to intercept on the first pass or completely prevent a throw-in within the time allowed. We switch on all crosses and all cuts, making our defense really a combination zone and man-to-man. We play to prevent the long pass. If the first pass is successful and a player is caught out of position, we use leap frog tactics along the side-line. The back player comes up cautiously to slow the dribble down and the out-of-position player races back to take his place. As he passes the dribbler, he sometimes attempts a steal by batting the ball to his advancing teammate; but he always remembers to get to the open man. Double teams take place only when the dribbler allows himself to be pinned against the sideline or center line. It can also take place when the dribbler stops and isolates himself near the center court. The two double-teamers then charge, hands held high and waving, feet wide. All pivot men are overplayed, with the off-side man ready to cover under the basket in case a high over-the-head pass to a pivot cutting for the basket is tried. (We sometimes get a charge call on this blind cut by the pivot.)

Sometimes we let the man guarding the toss-in play the middle and race for the interception on the throw-in.

We press after a foul shot, after a successful basket, or after a loss of the ball out of bounds.

If the press is unsuccessful and the offensive team gets the ball across the center line, we drop back into a 2-1-2 or 3-2 zone and begin our half court press from there.

Our second "press" is actually a mild two-man press with the guards contesting their ballhandlers, switching on all crosses. Our forward line has first formed a wide rebound triangle, then edged out to play for the long passes. If the press "gets tough," they go man-to-man all the way, hoping for a wild pass. This has been perhaps our best full-court defense. We "ease into it."

We especially work on two things with our defenses—both have to do with using the hands on defense. We do not teach the "one hand up and one hand down" defensive stance. We have our players use a "boxer's" stance, with both hands held in position to continually "stab" at the ball. We keep the dribbler worried about ball possession in this way.

Footwork and body balance is important, but recently we haven't had to worry about that much. Players have been able to compensate somewhat for lack of balance by terrific leaping agility and the ability to "pin the ball to the boards" or slap the shot away after it has left the shooter's hands. The use of hands to worry the dribbler is, we feel, the key to good defense. We tell our players to "take the ball." Sometimes they foul doing this, but that's better than timid play. After a while, the players get expert at it.

We teach a drag step for footwork and "we get there the fastest way we can," when a man is getting open. We don't worry much about crossed feet. That doesn't happen often with good players.

We also teach the use of forearms to protect the defense. Most modern dribblers are terrific drivers. They have to be stopped by powerful pressure, or they'll keep forcing their way into the basket. Strong forearms and solid hips will prevent that.

Anytime a dribbler edges by two of our players, we have one move behind him to slap the ball to his teammate and immediately cut for a return pass. That often gives us our fast break.

For the last two years our teams have been more successful changing opposing teams' tempos by pressuring on the half court. Our basic defense is man-to-man, but it begins with a 2-1-2 zone. From there we pick up individually, but always playing with zone principals. We sag on the off side, overplay for the long passes and play in front of the pivots under the basket. On all cuts by the guards, we "get in the way" of the cutter for three steps to break his rhythm. On cuts by forwards across the foul circle, we actually *prevent* by getting there first and forcing them to go around us.

We have our guards "point the ball," always putting pressure on the ballhandler. To compensate for this, the "next man over" plays "inside his man" (towards the ball) and one step back in order to intercept in case the dribbler breaks through. We do not allow the pivot men to handle the ball at all. If the ball gets to him, we immediately throw a charging "five-man zone" into him so he can't get rid of the ball. Alert action here can get plenty of steals. We don't go in, hands flailing. We run straight into the ball with hands stabbing at it. We may foul, but more often than not we latch onto the ball itself.

Our secondary man-to-man defense is a slight variation of the zone match-up which you might call our basic defense. (It isn't really a zone and it isn't really a man-to-man, but we prefer trying to convince our opponents to think we are zoning. Sometimes we even let the first cutter go through unchecked so he will think it's a zone.)

For variation, we have our three largest men form a rebound triangle close to the basket and pick up the man closest to them. Then we have our guards meet their ballhandlers at the center of the court. We "point" the ball, playing it closely, but drop the other guard back slightly to pick up the ballhandler in case he gets by the defense. Then the two guards merely change men and charge when the dribbler is off balance. Our center man on the rebound triangle prevents an "outlet" pass to the high pivot. Then, the closer the ball comes to the basket, the tighter we play it. Our guards retreat past the foul line to be in position for the high rebounds. We've found that by retreating all the way back, they often "lure" their ballhandlers in close. That's the best place to start our fast break from; no guard is playing back.

Using a Pressing-Switching-Charging Defense

On all our defenses we switch everytime two ballhandlers cross and we "charge" on the switches, being careful to "hold" the post man in so he can't roll for the basket. Even a slight bump against the post will often cause a bad pass. We've been lucky recently by having defensive men with quick hands latch onto most passes under the basket.

For under-the-basket play we teach our big men to position themselves "belly-to-belly." That's like face guarding, but the opponent often gets frustrated by such "sticky" tactics and moves completely out of danger territory. We contest his moves everytime he cuts for position. The inside men also switch and charge on all crosses. We tell our pivots to hold their hands out in order to "feel" any move by the offense, then contest it—"Don't let him go where he wants to go." Then when the ball goes onto the boards, "Block out, rebound and come down running."

We teach him to "tear" the ball out of a pile up. Sometimes we walk (with too much pressure), but most of the time we get out with the ball.

Our quick outlet pass is a great defense against guards penetrating too far. If the opposition dreads the fast break, they often stay back so far that the opposition has only a three- or, at most, four-man offense. We can double-team the ball under those conditions.

On special occasions we actually use a 2-1-2 zone, especially against throw-ins on the base line, but we quickly pick up man-to-man when the ball goes into play. Often we've found that against a zone, the opposition tosses the ball high and towards the middle of the court. If we're alert, we can contest the pass, often tip it on down the court, and run under it for an easy layup.

No team can play a fast-break game without playing an alert defense. Shoulders should always be squared with the end line, knees bent, back straight—a sprinter's position for the start! The first three steps either get you open or the fast break fails.

5

Keystone of the Patterned Fast-Break Offense– The Penetrating Guard

The penetrating guard is the key player of any great team—a guard who doesn't hesitate to penetrate the defense into the foul circle area. He is able to carry the ball inside the first line of defense to get 2-on-1 or 3-on-2 setups on the big men right under the basket.

The penetrating guard is certainly the key player on our team. Without his ability, we would have only the set-shot, rebound offense that so many high school and college teams boast of today. He's the secret of our success. We look for this man first of all on our team.

Guard's Characteristics

This man should be slender, fast and durable. He must have wide peripheral vision. He should be an excellent dribbler with a

49

good change of pace. He should be able to reverse himself with ease and be able to dribble with either hand. Above all he should be able to hit the basket from middle distances with a good, easy jump shot. He should be able to drive for the basket expertly on crips. He should be the best passer on the team.

His first weapon should be his outside shot; his second weapon should be good crip shots; his third, passing ability. No team can be of championship calibre without this good player. He's the "quarterback" of the team.

On the fast break, this man is usually on the receiving end of the outlet pass. We like to have our best guard in the center lane on the "three-lane" fast break. In fact, we pass up our second pass on our pattern if he does receive the outlet pass from the rebound. We have him dribble to the middle, the center man cross to the guard's original lane, and we run the break a bit slower to take advantage of the guard's ballhandling abilities.

If the break is 2-on-1, the penetrating guard usually drives and leaps before the pass-off to his teammate. He makes the defensive man *commit* himself, then he shoots or passes, whatever the situation calls for. The tighter the game, the more we want this player handling the ball; however, as we have said before, we don't want him "freezing" the ball and trying to do everything himself. He must realize this and be quick to take advantage of passing opportunities.

Then, above all, we want our guards taught to go straight down the court, penetrate to a good shooting position, and then let fly at the hoop with a jump shot. We make them practice this shot constantly and we make them take the shot in the summer months when they are playing on their own in pick-up games. In practice by themselves we make them begin their dribble at the center court, drive in a straight line for the basket and take the jump shot "from the same distance" as the curve of the foul circle. We tell them that distance never varies no matter what kind of court they are playing on, so to practice it like they practice foul shots.

The Guard's Shooting

Basically we work on shooting from five spots: straight down the middle; down each crip-shooting lane; and one yard outside each foul line on the curve of the circle (foul line extended). We caution them always to take the shot facing the basket with no fakes or no extra moves. They actually have little trouble getting open in games for this shot. Our troubles come only when they're missing.

On the half court our guard begins his hardest work around the key hole. He uses pivots and picks to free himself; he penetrates between the lines of a zone defense. We like for him to use two motions to get himself open from a sticky guard: the "rocker dribble" and elbow hook, and "reverse hooking pivot" with a jump shot or pass on the end of it.

These moves seem complicated, yet they're really relatively simple. They free a player from a hard-working guard's own efforts against him. The dribbler starts his motion, draws his defense with him *away* from his point of attack, then having "positioned" his defensive man, he "alerts" him with a quick rocker movement, freezes him with a hesitation, then makes a driving brush-off on a post or hooks him with his non-dribbling forearm and elbow to "hold" him behind our driving position. The guard then calmly forgets him and goes to work in an advantageous position on the next defensive man. His motion must be sharply efficient with no hesitation. That's what we call "balance." A fumble will kill the attack. If this happens, then the ball should be taken outside for another start.

The "reverse hooking pivot" is done when the court is cleared of posts and pivots. The situation is 1-on-1 with room to maneuver. The dribbler forces an overplay to one side, then he quickly reverses his dribble, spins, hooks his man behind him with a foot, thigh and hip, continues the dribble to the basket or takes one more dribble, balances himself by placing his feet in good position, then goes up for a jump shot or pass.

These two moves must be practiced to perfection by all guards if the basic fast break offense is to work.

Getting the Ball to the Open Man

After the moves, however, the "real" work comes. That work consists of getting the ball to the open man. The ballhandler must remain cool, calm and collected, yet able to shoot the ball to his teammate with no wasted motions and in a manner that he can handle the ball. If he does not pass the ball then he must be able to make those "little pot shots" and he must not miss.

Our penetrating guard helps us get the good shots, but since we have never had much trouble getting good shots near the basket, we don't waste long hours of work on half-court situations for this purpose. We work long hours, but our work is for the development of quick, efficient passes. To be able to do that, we must "know each other" by working those long hours. We then learn each other's weaknesses and strong points, learn to use our abilities to the best advantage and to bypass the weaknesses.

We come quickly down the court, penetrate to the good shooting positions and fire away, going after our own rebounds. We don't wait for our rebounders to get into position in a formal way. On our fast break, big men are suppose to get there about as soon as the opposition's big men get into defensive positions, so we figure we have an equal advantage with the defense, if we hurry even if we don't wait for rebounders. We hurry everything but our shots. We take our shots with a "1-2-3" count from around the foul circle. On our drives for the board, we try to keep our players from making "soaring glides" through the air. We've found a running defensive player is able to block those "holding" shots. We teach our players to "drive through" the back board on crips, to carry the ball all the way to the basket. When they shoot from "near" the board, leaping players often intercept them. Any attempt to block "drive through" shots will be goal tending or fouls.

Using Rhythm

We always take our shots within the "rhythm" of our moves. If we wait too long, the shooters become restless and nervous. After a while everyone becomes worried, so they usually wind up taking hurried shots that end up off their marks and in the hands of the opposition.

The only thing to do when that happens is to "balance the court," and start a pattern all over again so as to regain the rhythm.

Our guard always handles the ball on all out-of-bounds plays in the forecourt. He quarterbacks the play, then usually ends up the pattern on the receiving end of a pass for a shot from behind a screen. This way he gets his share of the points so at other times he's willing to pass off generously, making our team work better. Also, if he's covered by a frantic defense on that screen, he is the best man to get the ball to the open player.

We do not like for this guard to have to throw the ball in from the end line after a successful basket by the opposition. Too much time is wasted if he has to retreat from his defensive position around the foul circle, so we have our tall rebounders throw the ball in to him. If our fast break and our "secondary" fast break are to work, then there must be no time wasted in getting the ball back in play.

Guard on Defense

On defense we prefer to have our guard playing a man who likes to come in close to the pivot or post men on offense. That way he can double-team on the post and help prevent big men driving for the bucket on one-on-one situations. We like for him to "clog up the middle." If he is quick, he can steal the ball several times during the game to set up the fast break. In several games we have actually played a 5' 9" guard in the center position of our 2-1-2 zone defense. Opposing pivots became very nervous in their ballhandling after he made two or three steals. However, this young man could leap high enough to dunk the ball, so he was able to snatch the high rebounds with no loss of efficiency there.

Once we believed in and taught a "half court" game of basketball. We walked the ball down court and "set up" for half court patterns. We used forms of shuffles and various weaves. We spent hours learning the "back door" cuts and "swing" offenses. Then we found ourself one year with a couple of penetrating guards. We changed our style to a "full court" offense. We've concentrated on a game played "on the full court" ever since. We believe that's the way the game is supposed to be played. The athletes themselves will play it that way if you let them.

Certainly, we spend a lot of time on half court patterns. We run patterns until they become second nature; but we spend equal time on full court patterns. It gets results. There's no room for big, hulking, out-of-shape players in this game, however. Every player must be in prime condition and each one must be able to penetrate defenses on 1-on-1 situations. The key to this game is, of course, those good penetrating guards who know how to go for the basket and don't waste any time doing it.

Every national championship college team has guards like these. Experts who know the game will tell you the pros have them now. Once the pros used mainly giant players, but the winning teams are going to the penetrating guards now—those ballhandling speedsters who can play the full court, pass, run and gun from proper distances.

They make the game look unbelievably simple. They make it interesting. That's why the fans are flocking to the games as never before. And frankly, the game really is a simple one, providing the guards turn the ball loose at the proper time and in a proper manner. It's a game of "give and go." The penetrating guard can do it.

6

Full-Court
Patterned Break Offenses

Patterned fast breaks are basic. They don't seem to be difficult to teach; however, the difficulty lies in getting the players to run them the right way at the right time. Even in the pros a player sometimes latches on to the ball and doesn't seem to be able to turn it loose. Often he doesn't actually know he is holding the ball. This hurts the thing called momentum. If one player doesn't cut at the right time or if he cuts and doesn't get the ball, the pattern is broken up and momentum is gone. The offense begins to stumble, fumble and fall. Attempts at the basket are then taken haphazardly. Team morale is shot. That's when the coach calls time out in order to get his team together again. He often has to substitute for his best ballhandler, if that ballhandler is holding to the ball. So the ball must be released if the fast break is to work. Fast dribbling alone won't do it.

A fast-break attack can't be run without every player participating. If one player "dogs it" or rests on offense, then the pattern won't work. If the "rebounder" under the board won't stay back and play defense behind the fast break, then the opposition often has the opportunity to fast break the other way. The basics that make up the fast break are, of course, (1) the strong rebounder who can get the ball off the board and pass out well, (2) the ballhandling back court men who can pass well, and (3) the drivers who can go for the hoop when open. Those drivers must also be able to hit the little pot shots over a lone defender. Someone must grab one of the three lanes on the fast break everytime a break starts. Often a big rebounder will do this, coming in a bit late. With a slower timing he can often walk all the way in on the 3-on-2 fast break. Sometimes he is wide open, if the defense tries to play it man-to-man, as they often do.

We've found that our drivers must receive extra training on going for the boards. Inexperienced players often "run by" the boards, or take bad shots because they can't keep their bodies in line with the hoop. They often veer away from the true crip shot line, so they make a simple shot look hard. This seemingly simple maneuver must be practiced continuously. Too, crip shooters often hold the ball a second too long—even the best shots. They seem to want to shoot reverse layups and going-away shots when a simple crip will do. The driver must go all the way "through" the plane of the hoop and board, carrying the ball almost to the rim. Then the break looks simple, and the best breaks are rather simple. In fact, the whole fast-break system is simple. The answer lies in getting players to turn the ball loose.

For training drills we divide the court into four areas (see Diagram 6-1): (1) the "defensive" part of the court from the defensive foul line extended to the goal; (2) the passing area from the foul lane to the center line; (3) the "approach" to the offensive foul circle and (4) from the foul circle to the hoop. (Also see Diagram 6-2 for the three fast-break lanes.)

We play a "defensive brand of attack in" the number (1) zone. We play cautiously, don't make wild quick passes, often dribble out swiftly to the foul line. Then in area (2) we like to pass from lane to lane in order to keep the defense from setting up. Before we get through this lane to area (3) we like to have the

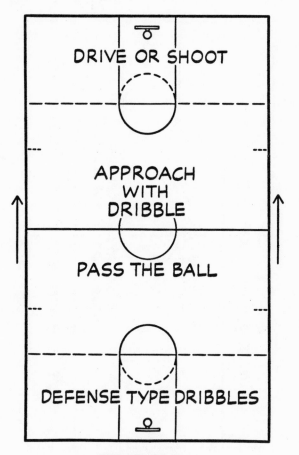

DIAGRAM 6-1

Court Divided Into Areas Of Expectations
As Far As Defense Of Fast Break Is Concerned

center man handling the ball and dribbling on approach to the circle. In area (4), passing is held to a minimum. We tell our players to dribble into the foul circle and take a jump shot. Then when he's up in the air he may find someone open to pass to. Everybody practices on this approach and jump shot until each player can hit spot-jump shots as well as he can shoot fouls from the foul line.

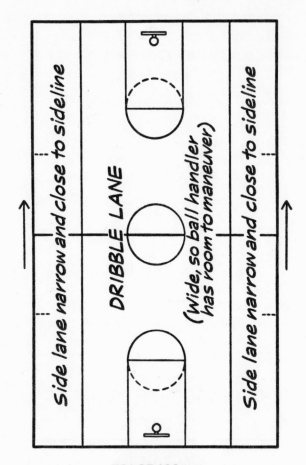

DIAGRAM 6–2

Court Divided Into Three Lanes For Normal Fast Breaks

Fast-Break Patterns

We use three simple fast-break patterns. We practice these breaks constantly from a zone style defense with our front men always leading. We are able to do this because of the half court defense we use. We always retreat after an offensive goal or foul shot to a 2-1-2 zone defense positioned close to the basket. Then we pick up man-to-man, always with our big men close to the basket, and our ballhandlers challenge their ballhandlers. We switch and charge on every cross-over and we slow our man down "three steps" on every cut through for the bucket. Then we switch with the big men closer to the hoop. That way we are always in position for the same type of fast break on interceptions or rebounds. Our basic fast break is an ancient pattern used by everybody, but with options (Diagram 6-3).

We split the backboard in the middle for the key to where

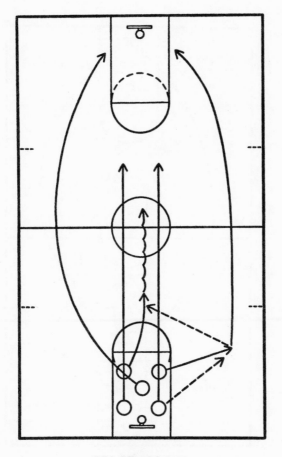

DIAGRAM 6-3

the first pass off the rebound goes. If the ball comes off the hoop to the right, the pass is to the right sideline; if it comes off to the left, then the left sideline. (If the ball rebounds off the front of the hoop and the center rebounds, the forwards spread, grab lanes and the center dribbles straight down the court.)

On the regular fast break, the rebounder starts his pass out. If, at the last moment, he sees a defensive man playing his pass, he hits the ball into the palm of his free hand and starts his outlet dribble (Diagram 6-4). This is a difficult and dangerous move. There is danger of a steal here, so he must literally "tear"

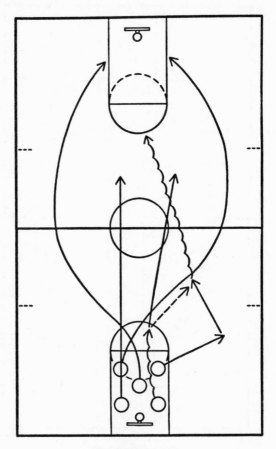

DIAGRAM 6-4

himself and the ball out of the pile-ups under the boards. He dribbles far out in front of his feet, reaching well out with the ball and "running through" it. Then he quickly hits the man on the same side as he intended to previously. This man has widened out and cut straight for the basket for a layup.

On the basic pattern, the outlet pass is made to the side near the foul line extended. The opposite guard then cuts across the middle for a short snappy pass. If that pass is being overplayed by the defense, then he bypasses this man and dribbles to the middle lane himself (Diagram 6-5). The cutter continues toward

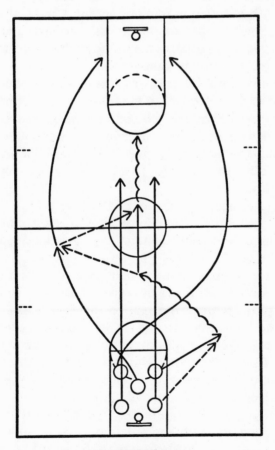

DIAGRAM 6–5

the side he is facing. As soon as the dribbler has hit the middle, we want him to snap the ball to the side cutter he is facing. The side man then drives straight for the basket.

The center lane is always filled by one of our good dribblers. Our center, who is also always a good ballhandler, always fills the off-side cutting lane, first *always cutting opposite the ball* on the outlet pass. He has to block out on forming the defensive rebound triangle on our goal, so he always comes in just a bit late. We expect him to do that and we make the pass to him with that in mind. A great part of the time he is the one to get the basket. Remember, we have our ballhandler approach the foul shot lane with the idea in mind of getting a jump shot. If he is challenged, then he passes in the usual triangle manner. The original rebounder and the last man down the court take up the defensive guard positions temporarily.

When no defensive man overplays a pass, we teach our middle man to drive straight to the foul line or to either end of it and *shoot a jump shot*. We tell him to *expect to shoot*. Then he doesn't have to worry about the timing on a possible pass. If a man is open, then he quickly gives him the ball for an easy crip. Psychologically, the plan to *shoot first* takes a load off the dribbler's mind.

We use a second fast break (Diagram 6-6), which is our "side line" fast break for play against a team that has been trained to jam the middle. The outlet pass is made to the same foul line extended position. The offside forward continues his cut, and takes the ball near the right sideline at mid court. The center cuts straight for the right corner to become the feeder. He takes the pass, returns the ball to the first guard cutting or (option 1) he fakes the pass, drives off the cutting guard to the front of the basket for a hook or jump shot, or (option 2) he feeds the offside rebounder who has cut down the far lane by the "back door." On option 3 he takes a shot at the basket with the cutters forming the rebound triangle, the last man down the court staying back on defense. This attack often penetrates into the scoring zone *around* a defense that is slow setting up. The basket is often scored before the defense can locate the ball.

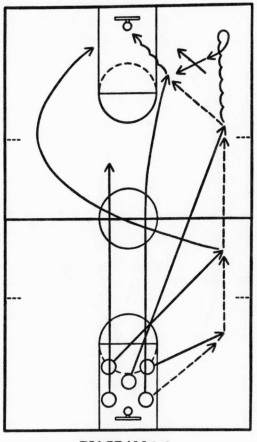

DIAGRAM 6-6

All the passes on this attack are "safe" passes that aren't likely to be intercepted. If the original attack is not successful, then the ball is returned to the area outside the foul circle and a regular half court pattern is run.

Our third fast break is called our "³/₄ speed break" or our "secondary" fast break (Diagram 6-7). Perhaps we fumble the ball, we miss an outlet pass and hold the ball, or we are slow getting the ball in from out of bounds. We are assuming our opponent's defense turns and slowly shuffles back down court.

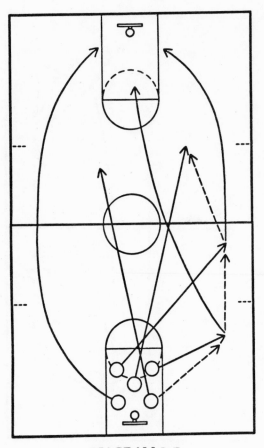

DIAGRAM 6-7

We do not wish to alert them so we hesitate a moment, then start a similar pattern to our sideline pattern. Cautiously we hit the center line so as not to awaken the defense, then we begin the all-out attack on the startled defensive players. We hold our pivot man wide on the side of the break, hit him quickly, have him feed one of the cutters down the middle and in the far lane. We also cut a man by the pivot on the right side, feed him if the middle is jammed, and have him drive the base line for a good shot or a feed to the other cutters.

Foul Shot Patterns to Break the Press
—for Simple Fast Breaks

We always line up two big men at the center line when we set up on defense for foul shots. They act as "wide pivots." We train them to "keep the defense on their backs" and to break toward the pass to prevent interceptions on the long pass. We often make our first pass, on missed foul shots or from out of bounds after a successful one, to these men rather high in the air, make them leap for the ball. Then they feed off to the ball handlers cutting down the side lines. One pass and a feed is often enough to get our dribblers ahead of the defense. Then it becomes a matter of two-on-one or two-on-two. We should be able to beat those odds. We "time" our pivots coming back to meet the pass and the cutters on the pass-off. The two passes to them should be about the same as a pass-lateral in football. There should be no wasted time or motion. The pivot then makes the inside roll, pivots facing the ball, steps wide and cuts straight down the middle for a possible return pass. The same attack is set up whether the foul is missed or made (Diagram 6-8).

If at any time the pattern is missed or if no one fills a lane, the ballhandler quickly dribbles to the middle lane. Everybody else clears out, grabs a cutting lane and the regular fast break is on.

Fast Breaks from Tips

We estimate our ability to gain the tip and set up our play accordingly. We use two simple tip plays—one offensive and one defensive. Our "offensive" tip is painfully simple, but we scored on it several times a game last year. Everybody knows how it works, but it continues to get points for us anyway (Diagram 6-9). The key is the timing on the break down court for the basket.

In center court and the back circle, we set up our "four corner tip." We release our fastest wing man completely, just as

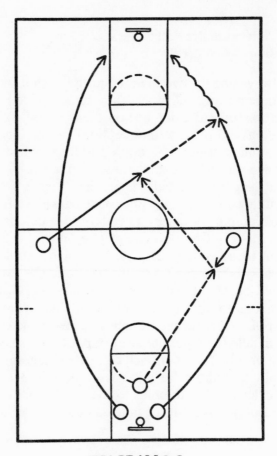

DIAGRAM 6-8

the official starts his toss. He breaks wide *toward the sideline,* then hard and fast for the basket, and outruns the defense. The ball is then tipped high over the head of the front "pivot" who is our tallest man. He brings the ball down, swings it into an *underhand* bowling-type pass to the cutter. We ask him to swing it underhand because many teams try to "jam" the pass by standing in the passer's way. A "swing pass" will get the ball around this man.

Sometimes two defensive men will contest the tip. If that

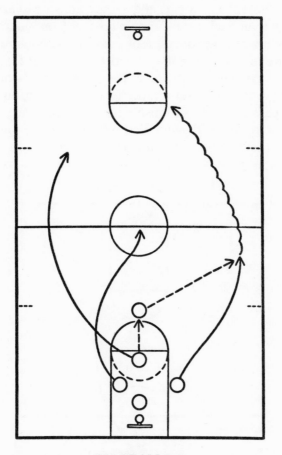

DIAGRAM 6-9

happens, and no one else is back, we ask our tall pivot to tip the
ball far down court and let our cutter break under the ball.
There's another little gimmick we use on this same play. We've
found that our jumper often tips the ball a bit too high and far, or
our "pivot" misses his timing and the ball is tipped just over his
head. In fact this has been done so often that we now always
delay-cut a second man from the opposit side, have him run
through the area where the over-tip may land. It's easy for him
to get the ball and pass it on to the forward.

Our "defensive" tip is the same setup as everybody else uses—one man back near our own goal with our guards blocking their men away from the area of the tip. The back man gets the ball. However, we are not satisfied just to get the tip (Diagram 6-10). We again cut a man just as the ball is tipped—again it's the off side man. The blocker on the right side widens out quickly to take the pass from the defensive man who has received the tip. He passes to the pivot who also widened out to the right. The ball is then fed to the cutter down the middle. If a defensive man is back, then the pivot quickly drives in the 2-on-1 situation.

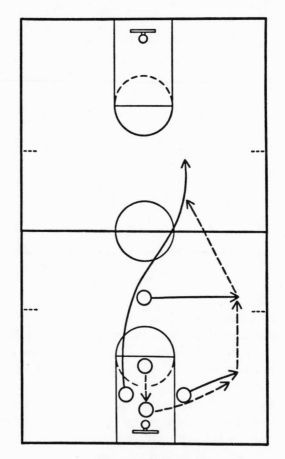

DIAGRAM 6-10

Two-on-One Fast Breaks

We also teach the "2-on-1" fast break (see Diagram 6-11). This break is so neglected we have often seen players in championship games automatically take the ball to the middle lane on quick interceptions enabling one man to guard two, when if he'd split the court like he's supposed to do, he could have walked right in to the basket. Often no one has a chance to grab the third lane on such a quick break, so a dribbler must

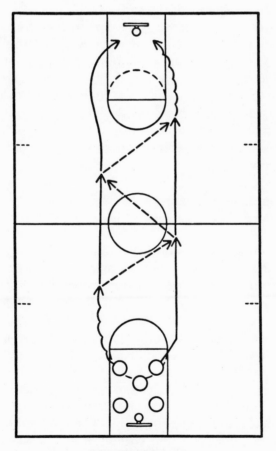

DIAGRAM 6-11

automatically divide the court up between himself and his teammate. In this situation we tell our players to make passes only at mid-court. When our two players have penetrated the main line of defense, we want the ballhandler to make a drive for the basket. We emphasize that a good player will carry the ball all the way to the basket and shoot and that a sorry ballplayer will chicken out and try to pass, sometimes walking with the ball against a sharp defender. That isn't always true, but a good guard who is outnumbered usually makes a fake at the dribbler at the critical moment then slides backward toward the other offensive man in order to intercept a possible pass. An experienced dribbler will walk right in.

The two-on-one offense is the opportunity for the two best ballhandlers to show their stuff. That's the reason we like to always have them up front on defense. They can steal the ball often by batting it away from a dribbler at key moments. One quick pass to the other usually gets them open. The key to their play is, of course, *anticipation* of the interception or the rebound and making the break hard and fast at just the right time. If they cut too soon, then the defense will drop back with them. A late cut is no good at all.

Luring Opposition into Mistakes to Open the Fast-Break Lanes

Experienced players do these things well. They learn them from playing with each other for many long hours with little supervision. In directed play it is possible and highly probable that they wouldn't learn them at all. "Alley ball" develops the individual play and the unorthodox styles so desired by colleges today. A "well drilled" team that has come up for years under a good coach wouldn't have sufficient individual skills today to combat a team that came up first under a "disorganized," unsupervised style of ball, where it's every man for himself, trained by a good coach who knows this style of play and welds the individuals into a cohesive unit. The "trained team" teams up well, but a cohesive unit without individual skills, unusual ability to get open on one-on-one drives, lacks real "attack" capabilities. It is with this in mind that we suggest the following "tricks" be encouraged and even emphasized. They should be used not for showboating but only when needed.

Experienced defensive players often allow the opposing dribblers to maneuver themselves into the offensive corners, then they just naturally double-team, cut off or intercept the outlet pass. They often force a jump or even gain control of the ball for a quick slash at the basket. Defensive players can also anticipate interceptions when one guard is driving for the ball. He quickly takes those first three steps down court to get himself open. If a player picks him up when he gets the ball, he often dribbles slightly away from the fast-break lane, drawing his man with him. Then he feeds the ball to a trailer cutting for the basket. A good dribbler leading the fast break in a 2-on-1 situation can often draw his man out of the play, then pin him to the sideline with a reverse hooking pivot while he feeds a wide-open trailer.

We've also seen a dribbler "tantalize" a defensive man into attempting a steal, then hook him with a pivot, bump him with his hip and continue to the bucket.

Another trick we often use is the between-the-legs dribble to get the dribbler open against a double-team by the opposition. We teach our dribblers to be alert for the defensive man who lets the dribbler go by him, then runs behind and slaps the ball off to a teammate. This double-team is good, often works. The facing guard gets the ball, tosses it down court over the head of his teammate who has slapped the ball and a quick basket ensues the other way. We counter this double-team by having our dribbler get ready for the attempt. When both guards go for the ball, he must change directions. If he reverse pivots, he runs right into the guard coming up from the blind side so we teach him to keep his feet far apart, and with a "rocker" motion to begin, dribble between his legs to change directions and go for the basket, leaving both guards behind him. He can in this way get two-on-one situations or three-on-two.

On a pressing defense from out of bounds under our own basket, we like to lure our man to the area right on the end line, then, using the body to pin him behind for the first pass. We take the ball in from out of bounds, lure the defense "behind" the ballhandler, hook him with a leg, and leave him with quick dribbles. We then go to work on 2-on-1 situations as they arise, always continuing full speed down court *all the way* to the basket. There must be no hesitation or fumbling of the ball. That would allow the original passers to catch up and we would lose our original advantage.

Keys to the Fast Break

Fast break patterns are easy to teach, but the keys to the success of the pattern are the two or three players who know exactly *when* to release on defense and cut for the boards on offense. They must not hurry, cut to soon, or else they will alert the defense to the danger. When they do make the move it must be at a time when the passer can get the ball to them in order to make the most of the advantage the cutter has gained with his first three steps. The first move must be not down court, but to "widen out." The cutter must always remember to look over his inside shoulder and to always face inward on the turn. We emphasize—*he must face inward.* There can be no fumbling hesitation or turning the wrong way. He must never take his eyes away, even for a moment, from the passer. In that split second when he turns his back, the pass is often released. He fumbles as he takes possession of it and the fast break is lost. At no time during the break must there be a drawing back to "telegraph" passes. Players must always *move the ball to the front man* no matter which lane he is in. He then regulates the attack to suit the oncoming cutters. The pass must be made to him from the position the ball is received. That way the ball is moved with speed and accuracy at the time the receiver is expecting it. The only time the pass is not made is when a defensive man overplays a pass. Then, without hesitation the ball is slapped into the palm of the loose hand and the player quickly dribbles forward, hits the cutter as soon as he has taken a couple of steps to get open.

The outlet pass must be quickly and efficiently made. If the rebounder or interceptor fumbles, he must quickly clear himself with a driving dribble. He must keep his head up and be alert to look for the cutter. The dribble gives his teammates time to "level out." Then he hits his choice of the one who appears to have the best chance of making the crip.

All our passes are *bullet passes*. We practice throwing and receiving them hard. We hit the receiver "where his hands are"—sometimes at the belt, sometimes near his head—wherever his hands are at the moment of the pass. We *do not lead the receiver*, we hit him where he is. We want to get the ball to him as quickly as possible. Then he can do what he wants to with it. The pass we throw is hard and swift, but it isn't a "heavy" pass that will make the receiver tighten up his hands to receive it. We merely want it to get to him in a hurry. We want him to receive it in a way that allows him to keep his balance and make the good play later.

All our players must play crouched and close to the floor. They have to have a good grip on the hardwood with the soles of their shoes. We want them to zip the ball around like a baseball player. We like one-hand passes better than two-hand snap passes, but we use either one when necessary. Without coiled muscles and firm footing the players can't zip the ball and they can't move quickly (as we say "like the big cat"). We don't care much about "bounding" ballplayers. It takes them too long to get down out of the air to be effective.

The fast break, to be effective, must have shooters who can hit the hoop about 8 or 10 feet from the bucket. Those are not long shots; neither are they crips. We call them little pot shots. They're hard to make, but if you have one player who can do it, then you've got a winner.

Fast Breaks Against Zone and Man-to-Man Presses

We don't spend too much time working against presses. We haven't had much trouble with those defenses for two years now. In fact, we play our best ball against them.

Frankly, we consider pressing defenses "sucker play." We

convince our boys of that. They don't fear presses at all; thus we have a psychological advantage. We figure that if we worked against zone and man-to-man presses for a long time, our players would begin to think they were extra special and fear them; so we merely vary our offense to bring our pivot men in a little closer, hit a pivot, break down the sideline for a return pass, hit the pivot cutting down the middle. We often find ourselves shooting layups.

We are simply providing "outlet" passes with our "wide" pivots. We then tell those pivots to get in the play by cutting straight down court. The system is unbelievably simple, mechanically perfect and impossible to stop by a pressing system that overplays the ball or wastes a player double-teaming. It enables our players to show their skills and proves the fact that no *one* defensive man can stop an expert dribbler.

Presses would work against a team that has one or two big rebounding goons who can't handle the ball or dribble, but not a team that has five good players, all of whom can do most anything with the ball.

It is our belief that full-court pressing defenses will be outdated within a year or so. The coaches themselves worried about presses so much they became a terrific psyhological weapon. Like Roosevelt said, "All we have to fear is fear itself." As soon as we get over that, presses will look silly to everybody. The key to the success of a press is an opposing team with guards who like to walk down the court dribbling slowly while their teammates seek positions with their backs turned to the ball.

The secret of our success against a zone press is the simple fact that we don't send anybody far down the court where one man can sag off, play two men for interceptions or the long passes. We pattern all five players in the back court, cut them to pivot positions, then have our men cut straight down court to outrun the two lines of defense. The pivot hands off, we "yo-yo" pass between the lanes, and we end up shooting crips wide open.

Fast Break Against a Simple Zone Defense

There are three things to remember in planning a successful attack against a zone defense: (1) You must beat the zone down the court. (2) You must plan a deliberate half-court attack against the zone to pull it out of position. And (3) you must be careful not to let the two distinctly different patterns run into one. The reason for this is, it's sometimes fatal to run down the court and quickly shoot against a good zone in perfect position. That means only one shot at the basket and no rebounds.

You must be careful to train your fast-breaking guards to realize just when the zone is in position. Then they must be patient, set up the deliberate attack and work for the good shot. If they continue on in against a good zone, attempt to penetrate a fresh, enthusiastic defense, they usually charge, walk or take bad shots with the big defensive players in perfect rebound position. So the fast forwards must realize, when the fast break is beaten back, or else all you are trying to do will work against you and the team begins to play "jitterbug" ball (that means, just running up and down the court at full speed, using a lot of energy and really getting no place). That's the time a coach has to take time out, settle his team down, make them see what they are doing, and change around a little bit so the attack will be more efficient. Great changes cannot be made during the course of the game. If they are attempted, we've found they often upset the equilibrium of the whole team and the game is sometimes lost through the actions of the coach himself.

If the zone is not beaten down court, then a deliberate attack must take place with plenty of "safe" passes around the perimeter of the defense to make the zone shift rapidly. We always keep two players back against a good zone, since both opposing defensive forwards always play between our passers for interceptions. If we have only one "point man" back and an interception takes place, the other team usually finds itself with a wide-open crip shot three or four times a game. Therefore, our deliberate attack against a zone is always some form of a 2-1-2 offense. We try to make the zone a "match up" affair. If we "overload" inside, their fast break is effective. If we overload outside, then we have no rebounder posted and their defensive strength sometimes proves to be too superior. So we "match up," pull them out and drive the zone for good shots, just as in a man-to-man defense. We try to pull them out of position, then pass to an open man for a quick jump shot, always remembering that the zone is a "sag-off" defense, hard to penetrate. The key to remember is that most passes are to be *around* the perimeter, and when the penetration is attempted, it must be made quickly and sharply with no slow fakes involved. It must be sharp as a rapier, with the ball carried quickly to release position.

Our fast break against the zone is in the same manner. All dribbles must be made straight toward the basket, with no slow-down permitted. As soon as the rebound or interception is made, we make our slash straight for the goal. We don't need many passes and those are made to get the ball quickly to the front man; then he drives, using only sheer speed dribbles. When he goes up for the hoop, he reaches quickly, beating the defense back. The first man drives all the way to the hoop; other breakers get the rebound positions. All passes near the basket are quick and sharp to players "coming back" toward the hoop. Fans like this kind of enthusiastic offense. They're often on their feet as it happens. Too, the players are enthusiastic themselves. They often want the ball again after the shot, and bounce into a sudden press to get it.

We have had some success in our fast breaks against a zone by working on the opposion's larger, slower players. We like to select rebounders who, while they aren't as tall and rough as some players we meet, are more agile and quicker to get down the court. We like for them to be good dribblers and ballhandlers, so we often select players who aren't over 6'6" tall in preference to the 6' 8" or 6' 10" rebounders. We then teach them to grab a lane and take part in the fast break. If we don't get the first drive at the basket, we have our taller boys—pivot men—go straight for the basket and *line up with the ball and the hoop*. If they do this quickly, then we often find our pivots playing against their little ballhandlers, while their big men are still coming down the court. A quick feed to them enables us to take advantage of the mis-matches. This happens often toward the end of hard-fought games when their big men become tired and don't react on defense with great enthusiasm. Then the opposing coach must substitute for them and our attack works well for the few minutes the new players take to "get their feet on the ground." Often the substitutes can be pressured into mistakes and the game broken wide open before the opposing coach realizes what has happened. Too, our regular attack goes better against men of less experience.

7

Three-Quarter Court
Patterned Fast-Break Offenses

This is our second most important attack—next to our full-court offense. Our philosophy here is to hit before the defense is set; to attack while the opposition is still looking around locating and organizing the team defensive play. It is our hope with this attack to take advantage of that player most teams have who can't locate his man on defense; of that player who makes his teammates angry because he won't get back down the court fast on defense; of that player who plays lack-luster defense, at best. All teams have those players; we try to locate them with this offense.

The ³/₄ court fast break does not wait for the defense to set up. Offensive players get to their positions easily, even before the defense is organized around the goal. The passes should get to them just as they arrive.

Ordinarily, slow-break offenses bring the ball down the

79

court to the area just outside the foul circle. The players are taught to 'balance the court" first, then to run offensive patterns. Today, a smart defensive player can pick out a team's pattern by the end of the first quarter. If the team continues to run those same patterns, it's easy for him to "play the play" and cut off the ultimate receiver. Often when that happens the good offensive player will take matters into his own hands, take simple free-lance shots from his favorite position. You see it happen in big-time college ball and in the pros every day. Patterns that won't work against smart players are discarded. If they aren't, then the team takes a beating. Any great offensive player is also quick to realize that, if his opponent is "playing a pattern," then he is also leaving himself vulnerable somewhere else. The offense must take advantage of this over-play. It is usually done by simply dribbling to where the defense basically should be and taking a good shot.

In our $3/4$ court patterns we have one guard move the ball quickly to the area just behind the center court circle. We space our three post men just outside the offensive foul circle and equal distance apart from sideline to sideline. The idea is to hit one of those posts and cut through for a return pass before the defense can settle around him (Diagram 7-1). The other posts cut straight for the hoop. Sometimes the post man who receives the ball is able to dribble straight into the basket. Frankly, no offensive pattern gets players open constantly against a good defense, but they do often get a player into 1-on-1 situations or get him open briefly for a good medium-distance jump shot. From there, we figure it's up to the player.

Our $3/4$ court offense explodes just before our guards cross the center line. The guard passes the ball around the defense by hitting one of the post men. He then feeds a man open near the basket, or he hits another pivot who gives the ball back to a cutter in an open lane.

The offense penetrates the lines of defense quickly and sharply without waiting for a pause that refreshes or a defense to collect in front of them. It explodes while the opposing players

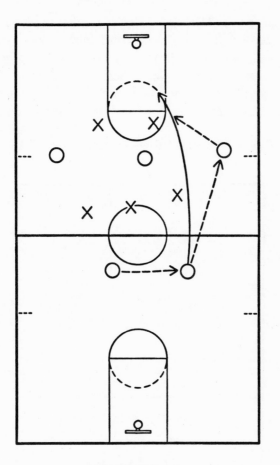

DIAGRAM 7–1

are still trotting down court, even before the defensive man has turned and squared his shoulders with the end line.

We wait for the sag-off or the double-team to become apparent, sometimes for the press men to begin to edge in, before we pass across the center line. Then we hit the off-side guard while he is still behind the center line, if the sag is away from him and towards the ball. He immediately hits the post ahead of him with a high, hard pass (no bounce passes for us).

As the ball nears the post men, the other posts make their sudden, sharp cuts straight for the basket for layups. They actually take an early jump. If either of them get a jump on the defense, we hit him with a sharp pass, and we have ourselves a bucket (Diagram 7-2). If the pivot man with the ball finds himself weakly guarded, he drives for the hoop, straight and hard (no fakes).

This offense is especially effective against a half-court zone

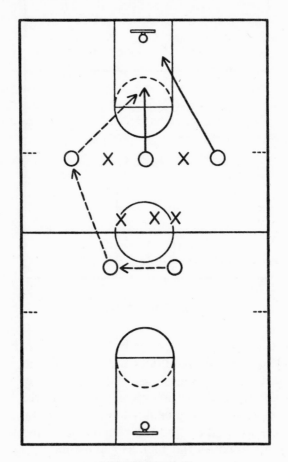

DIAGRAM 7-2

press or a half court man-for-man press. The tighter the defense is playing, the better these patterns will work. The closer a defensive man is playing, the easier he is to hook and block out of the play.

Variations

Sometimes our best attack proves to be a variation of this pattern. Immediately as the guards start their straight-for-the-hoop slashes, we have our post men reverse hook their defensive men away from the play, and keep them far outside. That allows no overplays, keeps the setups 1-on-1 or 2-on-2. We're confident we can score against those odds.

On regular sagging defenses we do about the same thing. We hold our side posts in the same wide positions across the center. We never dribble across the line. We pass to the wide men and cut the dribbler straight for the center where he rubs his man off on the post man. The side post feeds the cutter under the hoop. It's a fast pattern. Sometimes we also vary this by hitting the center (Diagram 7-3), cutting the wing men in by the back door. The wing men then cut straight across, and set picks for the guards who are then fed by the center. Our center thus must be an expert dribbler and driver. Usually by the time the guards have cut, he has faked his man out of position and driven for the basket.

These ³/₄ court fast-break patterns are crowd pleasers. There is no time wasted in getting men into set positions. Our players do not have to hold their fingers up signalling a play or calling out a number.

The screens take place further out, leaving the basket area open for drives. The feed-off takes place further out, as does the inside roll of the post men. These offenses usually end up with the floor men driving for the bucket and the big men rebounding the shots or tipping the missed crips back in. The angles of their cuts are the same as the fast-break lanes, so a covered dribbler knows where to pass. A man is usually there. The full-court

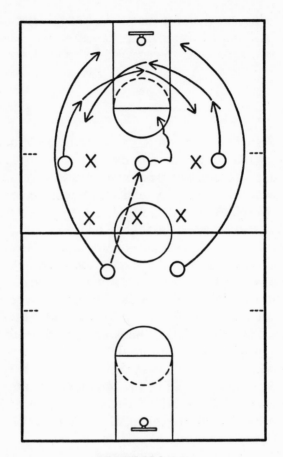

DIAGRAM 7–3

game and the ³/₄ court game are the only situations where our guards drive all the way to the hoop. On our half court game, the plan is to get our shots from medium distances behind posts or screens.

Use of Big Men

Our fast-break patterns on the full, ³/₄ court and even half courts move so fast, we have to give special consideration to the play of our big men who have to run from goal to goal, rather than from foul line to foul line like most little guards in ordinary play. If we use a very tall man, we always keep him back on the fast breaks (sort of a goal tender). The fast break will be completed before he gets anywhere near the basket, so we play him back in the forecourt, or use him for outlet passes in case we get into trouble. We also teach him to retreat all the way to the basket on defense, in case of interceptions by the opposition. He goes straight for the basket. However, on offense he stays back near the center of the foul lane until he sees what is happening. If he gets much closer, he'll get in the way of our ballhandling offense, which is at first a driving offense. Then, when the fast breakers see they can't make it, they toss the ball back to him. That is the signal to go into our half-court patterns. And our big man goes into his regular pivot position. That also signals certain changes in our defensive style of play, too. Our "second" pivot man, who always plays around the high post position near the top of the foul lane, now assumes new defensive duties. So do the guards. They now have the added responsibilities of "balancing the court" (without even thinking about it) and of keeping one man back at all times, behind the pattern for an emergency outlet pass. He plays completely defensively while his ballhandling teammate is cutting for the basket. He cannot go to the hoop, no matter what happens. We depend on him to be our defense. Our philosophy is, if he goes in, then nobody is back at all. The opposition can literally waltz to a basket on sudden interceptions.

If we play two big men, we always play them wide near the foul circle or foul circle extended, along with a third forward on this offense. They act as "posts" and handoff, but cut for the basket occasionally. On the half court patterns, we play our big men in regular positions, but we watch them carefully as they get up and down the court. They tire easily, so we substitute for them frequently. In fact, we've found in our style of play that a player 6'6" tall, who is mobile and a good jumper, is much better for us than one much taller. We put a premium on jumping ability rather than height.

We "take care" of our big men in other ways, too. We don't worry too much about the offensive tips after a foul shot since the defense already has position, so we use an agile tipper, not our big man. We set up for the offensive foul shot by stationing our big man back at the opposition goal on defense. He can rest back there, be ready when the offense comes down and our little men can take a chance or so at stealing the ball, assured that he's always in position behind them. They also know that they have to retreat all the way back to the basket on defense when we are playing our half court patterns. They know our big men can't get back fast, so they take care of them temporarily. We also teach them to help out on posts and pivots, since big men don't often have quick hands for steals, so they sag on the offside, worry the opposition's big man so he can't pivot freely with our big man behind him. That also sets our little men up for the fast break on interceptions. We try to make our $^3/_4$ court offense a "continuous" offense. We want to play full-court basketball all the way.

Pressure on Defense

Knowing that set patterns don't really mean too much; that " general" patterns and philosophy of team play means more, we try and instill in our players the fact that we need to keep "continuous" pressure on the defense. We try to do that even when the officials have to handle the ball on the out-of-bounds plays. We run all the time. We don't want any of our players resting at any time, either. We want all five players in on every play. We want them filling into proper positions, doing it instinctively instead of all jamming up in one pile under the basket, waiting for the ball to be brought down. Therefore, we give our front line wider positioning, have them handling the ball further out and assisting our ballhandlers to get the ball under where they can use their skills and abilities fully on drives for the basket. That's where it really counts. We repeat, *we attempt to get all five players in on every play.*

The patterns we have diagrammed for our $^3/_4$ court offense do that. Our players move *without* the ball. They don't "just move," however, with no real purpose. They work on "timing" and they work within the limits of the team play. They don't take over anyone else's positions, but they do take advantage of a teammate's laxity if he fails to move. Five men are always ready and close enough to the ball to do whatever is necessary.

We never like to have our team all spread out to the four corners of the court with the ballhandler isolated. We want our players all together within passing distance of the ball. Our $3/4$ court offense keeps the players together, and has them running patterns near the middle of the court, ending up with quick sudden slashes right at the basket. *All the players advance with the ball.* For this series the usual front line and back line patterns are inverted. The guards are playing forwards and the forwards, guards. The forwards are stationed so they have to play defense a bit. Frankly, they enjoy doing this since they aren't usually allowed to do it. It's a humpty-dumpty offense that really works.

The only real difficutly we have coordinating our different court patterns is changing from full, to $3/4$, to the half court without delay. All five players have to know what they are doing. If they *"Learn to play within the limits of the area around the ball"*, then we have a beautiful, *full-court* offense even when operating on the half or $3/4$ court. It's a *pressure offense.*

8

Half-Court
Patterned Fast-Break Attacks

We've found that perhaps our greatest challenge in running the fast break is to convert from full-court patterns to half-court patterns without loss of effectiveness. Too often players waste time "setting up." Too often they chicken out on drives they could have made. Too often they try drives they have no chance of making. Too often they make good moves and everybody else stands around—nobody helps them by getting themselves open. Too often nobody plays "without the ball."

The only answer we can give to these problems is: That's what you're working on—coordinating a team attack so that the offense works on all five cylinders. It takes a lot of playing together in game situations to make these important parts fall into position. It takes a long time to train players to know when to drive or shoot and when to hold up. Here, too, the answer we have given previously is the same—a player who turns the ball loose at the proper time and other players who cut sharply at exactly the right moments—the penetrating guards. These things have to be practiced so often and so long, they become second nature. When it does, the players love to play together. They don't have to think at all. It just happens. It takes hours of drill in competitive situations for the passes and cuts to come just right.

With that in mind we don't give our players a lot of plays to learn. They get mixed up when they have to think about what pattern we are using, so we use only four half-court "continuity" offensive patterns over the season's play. We have found these to be adequate for any defenses we have encountered. We use them with slight variations against both zones and man-to-man defenses.

Give and Go Offense

Our basic offense we call "give and go". It has (1) a cutting guard, (2) moving forwards, (3) rebound strength, (4) set shot opportunities, and (5) all the passes are "safe" passes—around the defense; yet we have (6) penetration, and (7) we drive the defense closer to the basket so we can get the good percentage shot. It also (8) forces the defense to one side and swings the ball to the other for an open shot. That's about all you can expect an offense to do. We use a three-inside, two-outside pattern (Diagram 8-1) starting from good balance with our pivot man under the boards and our wing men along the base line about half way out towards the side-line. We don't really want them to play that deep, but we start our pattern that way.

Starting with the single pivot man, we first break him to the center of the foul circle to receive the ball and a "split the post" action ensues, if the middle is not jammed. The wing men take the places of the guards. We do not really expect to get this easy pattern often, so our real pattern begins a split second later when the wing men break to the middle of their side courts—all the way to the foul line extended. A forward receives the ball and the passing guard cuts straight through to the basket. The center screens the off-side wing, who cuts in just behind the guard; then the center breaks back to the high post position on the curve of

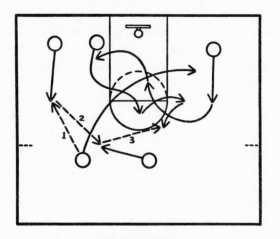

DIAGRAM 8-1

the circle *away* from the ball. If the ballhandling wing man is unable to hit a cutter or drive behind one, he returns the ball to the off-side guard who has taken the place of the cutting guard. The guard then swings the ball to the pivot who has the option of (1) shooting, (2) passing to the cutting guard, who has placed himself for a good-angle, medium-distance shot at the hoop, (3) hitting the low post who has lined up between him and the basket, and (4) driving for the basket. Thus the center keys our attack around the foul circle.

The ball is moved to the center with easy passes where the pivot actually has a good 1-on-1 situation for a jump shot at the basket, if nothing more. Not too much action takes place, but it is our theory that not much action is necessary, providing the front line men know how to get and keep their men "on their backs" (using their hips, elbows and bodies to screen their men behind them). When no shot is taken and the continuity has run its course, the pattern begins easily again from either side. We like to swing it from side to side to get better balance.

There are several other advantages to this setup that aren't apparent to the inexperienced eye. (1) Defensively one man is always back, but the original ballhandler is taking the pressure off himself by cutting for the basket. An overplaying guard thus finds his man sometimes walking right into the basket. (2) We are able to play our best man in the pivot position where he is stationed properly to get the ball *inside* and in a scoring position. He is also able to move outside quickly to act as guard or ballhandler if an emergency arises. (3) The two big forwards break into the low post positions where their height can prevail, yet they are also feeders from overhead passes, and if they are a bit awkward, they are usually out of the way on good drives for the basket by our best ballplayer. They come in strong just behind him to work on the rebounds. (4) This pattern also wheels the ball around a zone defense for a quick shot at the basket by a good guard after the zone has been pulled out of position. (5) The wing men do not play so deeply that they are caught out of the play on defense and become not much more than spectators flagging the play from behind. They are positioned so they often are able to intercept an opposing fast-breaker on his way to the basket. Sometimes our tall men are able to pin the ball to the boards after a long run and a leap at the opposing player's shot, or they are able to slap the ball away after it has left the shooter's hands. Our players like to do this, so we encourage them. Fans like it and it annoys the opposition who expect a clear shot at the basket.

Pro Set Offense

Our second continuity we call "pro-set" (Diagram 8-2). We use it basically to get the ball to a guard close to the basket; then we clear out, leaving him in a 1-on-1 situation. The formation is the same—two guards outside and three men on the front line. Passes are all careful and screens are set up both for the ballhandler and the off-side forward. They are moving screens. The movement of the ball is good, but this offense is basically for a team that has only one or two fine ballhandlers. We use this set up to vary our attack against teams who know us well.

The ball moves first on a screen from guard to guard. The guard then hits a forward at the foul line extended about halfway to the side-line. The forward immediately flips the ball back to

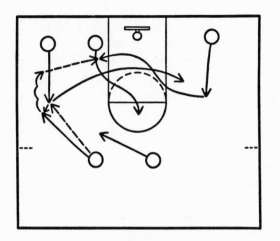

DIAGRAM 8-2

the guard who has cut to a spot behind him. The forward then starts to "go away" towards the opposite side of the court where he will set up a screen for the off side forward.

As he moves, the driving guard may (option 1) use him and his guard to pick his man off on a drive for the basket. If he delays, then (option 2) he hits the off-side forward who breaks to the low post and lines up between the ball and the basket. If the guard cannot get the ball to the post, he dribbles across court (option 3), brushes his man off on the high post and takes a jump shot or works the inside roll with the pivot. He has another option on his dribble across the court (option 4): the other guard cuts by him in the opposite direction. If the dribbler wishes, he can hand the ball off. Dribbler 2 then takes the ball all the way behind the low post man for a jump shot. Using these two options varies the offense so no one can over play the pattern.

We especially like this pattern against a man-to-man defense. The pattern is set wide so there is little chance of double-teams. The movement is good and there is always opportunity for good rebounds. Also there is little chance of interceptions that would end up with the other team shooting crip shots.

Sometimes we vary this offense by making it a three-man

outside weave, with two post men playing outside the foul lanes and half way out to the foul line. We break the post men a little higher, have them again return the ball to the dribbler and then clear out. He delays his screen for a second or so to give the dribbler time to drive on his man. If this does not develop, then both pivots explode for the basket at the same time after they have widened out. One may be open. If not, then thze pattern is started over again.

Carolina Four-Corner Offense

Against sticky man-to-man defenses and near the end of the game when we are leading and need to freeze the ball or swap the clock for a basket, we use our "Carolina four-corner" offense. This is basically a pass-and-go-for-the-basket type of offense (Diagram 8-3) set the width of the court. We let three men do most of the ballhandling, with the other two returning quickly to corner positions after their cut.

No one moves until the ballhandler makes his first dribble. Then the man he's facing makes a fake at the basket, comes back to receive the ball. He then "freezes" where he is (without

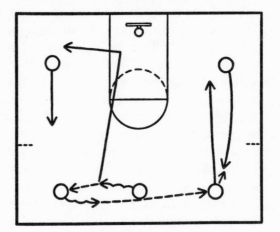

DIAGRAM 8-3

making a dribble) and by doing so he also freezes his defensive man into a stationary position. He may hold his man with a move of his front foot or a fake of his shoulders. As his defense finally starts towards him, he begins his dribble across the court and several feet away from the center line. When he begins his dribble, his teammate facing him makes a fake for the basket, comes out for the ball. If his defensive man is pressing him too closely, he turns and sets up a screen for the corner man on his side who breaks all the way out to take the ball. After each pass the player who has released the ball cuts all the way to the basket. (We emphasize "all the way" because sometimes the cutter is prone to go about half way to the boards, then angle off to the corner. Sometimes a long pass to him at the last moment goes needlessly out of bounds under the boards.) The dribbler crossing the court can also reverse himself and go the other way. We must caution: Players must not be allowed to "edge in" close to the ballhandler. They must stay wide and away from him until he makes his move. Then they must cut sharply for the position to take the ball. Again the ballhandler must freeze his man into position and the pattern repeats itself. If the players are patient, one of them will be wide open after a little while. Just wait for someone to make a mistake. When he does, get the ball to the open man. No one is there to help the defense.

This offense is sometimes so good we've often thought of using it as our basic offense against a pressing man-for-man defense. Our fans often call for it when time is running out and we are leading a good team by a few points. The opposing fans boo when we go into it, but they respect it. It's a "keep away" brand of ball that preserves a lead, but it often increases the lead, too. It's hard to combat.

Last Shot of the Quarter Offense

Our "last shot of the quarter" offense (Diagram 8-4) is a three-man weave on a double post. We time ourselves for an 8-second start. That gives us the weave, the shot and a possible rebound. The point man takes the shot. He starts the weave opposite the area where he is to shoot. The second man to handle the ball hands off, then sets up a double screen with the pivot. On the third exchange of the ball, the dribbler drives behind the screen and takes the shot. The opposite pivot takes his rebound spot, the on side pivot takes the middle, and the screening guard takes the third rebound spot. The remaining guard stations himself in the foul circle for an outlet pass and shot or a high rebound. We want the shot taken by a shooter who naturally jumps high before he releases the ball. That way there's little chance of it being deflected.

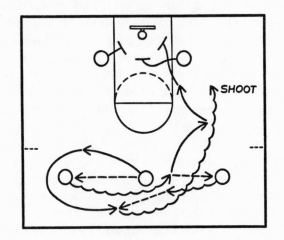

DIAGRAM 8-4

9

Special Situation
Fast-Break Patterns

Believing players should know what to expect in every situation, for all eventualities. One out-of-bounds continuity (Diagram 9-1) is all we use for sideline plays, but it has many options. We use it in both the forecourt and the backcourt. The only difference is we set up much wider for the backcourt. We have the same ballhandler take the ball out of bounds. He hits the other guard (if this guard is pressed he may screen the offside forward, have him take the ball and, changing assignments with him, temporarily run the forward assignment). The ball then penetrates to the pivot who breaks up the lane on the side where the play begins. The onside forward then screens the player who has tossed the ball in and we begin the "Kentucky guard around" play.

It is basically split-the-post. After the pivot man receives the ball he has five options. The first option is for him to hit the guard cutting from the out-of-bounds spot down the sideline for

97

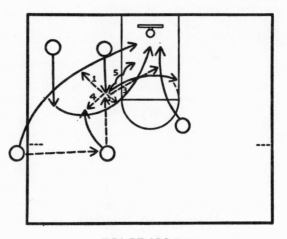

DIAGRAM 9-1

the basket. Timing must be perfect here. The ball is handled on fingertips *over the head*— this means from the pass in to the pivot. A delay or fumble will ruin this pattern; even a fake will ruin the timing. The pivot man plays his natural style. The second option finds the screening "on-side" forward cutting behind the pivot across the middle. The third has the original guard, who has thrown the ball in, breaking on across the foul lane to draw his man on out of the way. The forward cutting across then changes direction and sets a screen for the offside forward who cuts off the screen for the hoop—not behind the pivot man. The fourth option finds the guard who has remained outside coming behind the pivot for a jump shot; and fifth, the pivot man drives for the hoop.

This continuity should be run by all players doing exactly the same thing every time the ball is tossed in, no matter what happens. The cutters time themselves with the pivot man's motions. The pivot swings the ball, protected between his knees, according to the following cuts: (1) toward the side-line cutter, (2) then the flip pass to the screener cutting behind him, (3) to the off side forward, (4) to the back guard (5) drive. The moves are always the same.

If we run into a pressing defense, we use this same series

from the backcourt. We merely widen out to do it. No man-for-man defense over the whole court can stop it without plenty of switches and sags.

Sometimes we have difficulty in getting the ball to our pivot man because of overplays on him. When that happens, and no man is sagging off to cover him from the rear, we merely have the pivot pin his man behind him with his hip and elbow and hold his free hand out to where he wants the ball, always reaching for the basket. We give him a little lob pass. This is usually enough to discourage the over-play. We emphasize to the players *that this lob pass must take place.* We do not want the pivot man bothered by overplays later in the game. The defense must be whipped into position early, if our fast break patterns are to work. (We also take advantage of other over-plays on other patterns the same way—and we emphasize we *must take that advantage* so the defense will see its own mistakes and won't try the same tactics again.)

If it is impossible to get the ball to the pivot or if the defense is playing a zone against us, we vary the pattern a bit as to where the ball goes, but our players run the same pattern as always (Diagram 9-2). We don't hit the pivot against a zone; we pass the ball in the same way (over the head) to the guard. He fakes to the

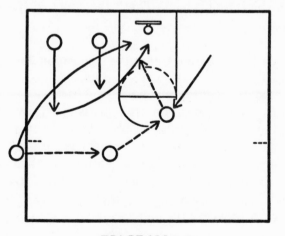

DIAGRAM 9-2

pivot, then throws to the off side forward who feeds the opposite forward cutting off the pivot man just like in the original setup. He hits the forward with the ball *just before* the cutter breaks free of the lane. By hitting him early, the cutter is able to see where he is going and to make a good move. If the ball is passed to him late, he may have to hurry his shot and actually miss a wide-open crip. *Getting the ball to him just before he breaks clear* is the secret of this maneuver.

In the original pattern we have to caution our pivot man not to pass to the first cutter if he does not get the ball quickly and sharply. Any delay will cause him to toss the ball out of bounds behind the guard. The second hand-off also must be to the screening forward (who cuts off his own screen) *before* he passes the pivot man. This must be done to keep him from charging on a switch by the defense, and to enable him to work efficiently on the inside roll with the pivot cutting down the middle on the switch. The off side forward must be taught to "go to sleep" over on his side so as to allow his man to relax. Then when the time comes for the screen to take place, he "explodes" straight toward the basket.

The center, when he gets the ball, has that option of exploding for the hoop *whenever* he finds his defensive opponent "playing the passes" or dropping back and "watching." He must keep his man alert on his back. That's the way to do it—explode at any time.

Out-of-Bounds Patterns from Under the Opposition Basket

Many coaches feel there is no reason to run a pattern from this position if the opposition isn't pressing. They have one player toss the ball in, the other dribble the ball down the court. We do not allow this to happen. The reason is partly psychological. We've seen too many players who felt it was their only duty to "escort" the ball down the court. They wanted to do this. It satisfied their vanity of performing in front of the crowd. They always ran back to where the ball was to be tossed in, held their hands out for the ball; then they wouldn't turn it loose until they had "walked the ball" across the center line. The other reason is that it isn't good "full-court" basketball.

We do not allow a player to dribble the ball down the court unless he's doing it in the fast break at full speed. Often while the dribble is taking place the forwards and center are trotting down the court with their backs to the ball. Nothing can happen until they turn around. If the guard tries to force the play he usually loses the ball by an interception or a toss out of bounds. Also when a half-court press takes place, all players need to be alert. It sometimes takes a startled yell to awake them to the fact that a guard is in trouble. We have found a fast-break pattern that keeps them alert and penetrates quickly so as to keep the defense always alert.

We usually bring the ball down the right side of the court, but either side will do. The forward on the right side waits for the ball just across the center line in a wide post position somewhat near to the foul line extended. The center cutting down the middle times himself to go just about the time the forward receives the ball. If a play cannot be made, the center screens the off-side forward who then breaks across, lines himself up with the basket and the ball in a low post position. The center then comes back to the high post; the guards come across the middle line and our ordinary $^1/_2$ court offense goes into operation. No one can go to sleep or rest a bit in this kind of pattern. It keeps the pressure on both teams and our would-be dribbler has to satisfy his ego in another way than merely dribbling the ball down court. His achievement must be real.

Out-of-Bounds Plays Under the Basket

Again here, we don't waste too much time working on these patterns. We learn them, then we work on *making* the players run them during games. We don't care to have an out-of-bounds play that is satisfied with merely getting the ball in bounds. With everybody alert and the timing set with the first pass, it should be easy to work out a pattern that is impossible to stop. The shot may be missed, but no one can stop a shot that has five players working to get it.

We use three simple patterns here (Diagrams 9-3, 9-4, and 9-5). Diagrams 9-3 and 9-4 are "swing" patterns, since many teams prefer to zone on throw-ins under their own hoop. On both patterns we line our players up "4 square" along the foul lane. At the given signal of the slap of the ball, the four players rotate going toward the basket on the side of the ball and away from the basket on the opposite side. They merely move "one man" around the square and take up the position of the player ahead. If no one is open, another move around is made on a second slap of the ball. As the ball is tossed in, the player who did the tossing cuts along the base line to a position behind the post man opposite him. The ball is then wheeled *around* the defense to him for a good jump shot. Against an over-play, we change our pattern once in a while to a simple toss-in and a return pass just behind the receiver.

Diagram 9-5 was put in for easy shots under the basket. Too often everybody turns, looks for a wide cutter and forgets about the close players already standing under the basket. It is our idea

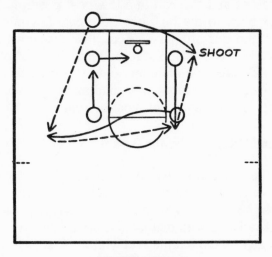

DIAGRAM 9-3

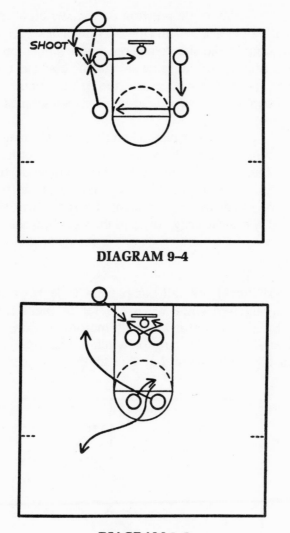

DIAGRAM 9-4

DIAGRAM 9-5

to get the players to look here first and hand the ball in for easy opportunities; then if they aren't available, to pass the ball outside on an "outlet" pass to a safety man. The play is a simple criss-cross of the two big pivot men under the boards and a cross of the two outside men. One pivot man screens the other, then reverse rolls to the inside position on the switch of the guards. He is usually open for a crip. One outside man screens the other who breaks out to the side to a good shooting position; the other guard then retreats to the same side of the court as the ball, but very deep. The player who passes the ball in breaks around the pivot men to the center rebound positon. Sometimes he's open for a pass and shot.

We also use another play when the pressure is man-to-man and tight. We line four players, one behind the other, in a row down the foul line. We break the first man wide to the left, second wide to the right, third high left, and the fourth man charges straight down the open middle for a crip shot. It's a specialty play we use only now and then on unusual occasions.

Inside Roll

A basic "must" for all our players to learn is the "inside roll" (Diagram 9-6) since we use a lot of picks that require switches by a team that is basically man-for-man. Once upon a time, players would not dare to switch and charge into double-teams on the ballhandler, but due to the quickness of hands

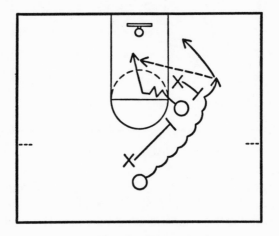

DIAGRAM 9-6

today, they are able to do so and get away with it, often before the dribbler is able to get rid of the ball. We work on this maneuver more than any other phase of the game today. This double-team off the screen is difficult to combat. That's why we let our players dribble between their legs, when this happens, to change directions. We also teach them to reach far out in front to get the ball to the open player, left so by the double-team. If we are able to do so, we are open for a quick basket.

We tell our post man that when the switch takes place, he must pivot facing the ball, get his man blocked out with a hip, and step first to widen out, then go for the hoop, balanced and with hands up for a quick pass. He must be able to reach for the ball quickly, for it may not be possible to give him a perfect pass. In fact, the victim of the double-team may have to leap into the air to get the ball away. The key to remember here is the pivot *facing* the ball and the first step to *widen* out away from the ball so one man can't guard two. The pivot man must then carry the ball close, keeping his eyes down until the last second before the release of the ball. Only then does he "locate" the basket. We tell our players to keep their eyes at medium height—"the hoop won't move."

Center Tips for Patterned Fast Breaks

We line up in a "four corner" setup (Diagram 9-7) with our tallest man up front toward the basket, two fast wing men on either side and our best defensive man lined up toward our goal. The ball is tipped to the front man who brings the ball down to his knees and "swings it" to the fastest guard who has released and cut from his wing spot as the referee begins his move to toss the ball. The cutter then drives for the basket. A secondary cutter from the opposite side delays just a bit, then cuts behind our tall man up front who is supposed to receive the tip. This is just in case of an "over tip" due to bad timing. This often happens, so the cutter merely takes the ball and feeds it to the front man from the center lane. The jumper cuts in the offside lane; one man stays back for the possibility of interceptions.

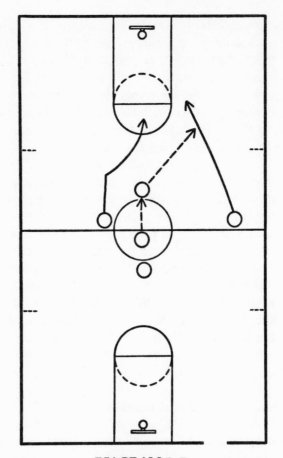

DIAGRAM 9-7

Our second tip play is in case we can't outjump the opposition. If we have a chance of tipping the ball by getting a hand up in front of the opposition on the ball, we tip it straight behind to the defensive man (Diagram 9-8). He then tosses it to the wing man who has widened out, and he moves it on to the center who also has widened out. The offside wing man cuts down the middle for a pass and a layup.

Remember, the key to this maneuver is timing on the break. The *cutter is released* just a second *before* the toss, not a moment

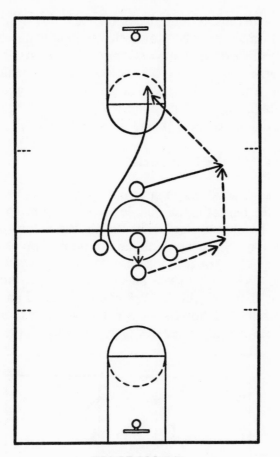

DIAGRAM 9-8

later. He must go at top speed. He must not wait for the ball. If he goes, he will be wide open two or three times a game in spite of how often the opposing coach has warned his players about the move, or how he tries to combat it. If he uses two men to press our receiver then—since we have our tallest forward in the front position—we tell him to forget about swinging it and to merely tip the ball on down the court to the man breaking. We warn him, however, not to tip unless *both* men are on his shoulders.

If one defensive man drops far back down the court, our fast-break man merely slows up a step and waits for his teammate to work the 2-on-1 offense or he "leads" his man over to the corner, reverse pivots, hooks his man behind him and feeds the trailer. Fans look for this play. It's good for some fancy dribbling and ballhandling at top speed. The players like it. It enables them to show their skill in pass work.

Tips at the Offensive Foul Circle

We set a good big man at each side of the lane with their backs to the basket in the double pivot position. The one on the left must be able to hook left. We tip the ball to one of them (Diagram 9-9). Since he is already in perfect pivot position, he shoots a quick pivot or hook shot. We do not want a dribble or fake here. We want to use sheer speed to get the ball away, exactly as if the player had rebounded, twisted and stepped to clear himself. The hook shot is actually better than a reaching pivot here, since the defensive man is already on the pivot man's back.

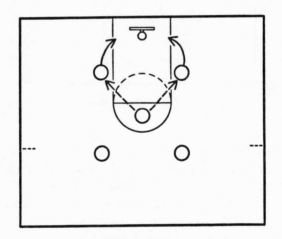

DIAGRAM 9-9

Special Set-up on an Offensive Foul Shot

We have found that our largest men often have trouble getting back after an offensive foul shot and setting up for defense, so we place our tallest player down the court near the middle line where he can quickly retreat to a goal tending position on a fast break or he can intercept a long pass to a "snow birding" forward. The defense already has the inside positions on foul shots, so we need more maneuverable players for the rebound. We need offensive "tippers" placing the big man back *before* the shot enables us to stop the fast break without too much trouble. A big man under the basket is a good psychological deterrent, no matter whether he can play good defense or not. We use one who can slap the ball away after a shot. He loves to do this and the fans love it, too, so after a slap or so the opposing forwards begin to look for him and don't operate as freely. This also gives our speedy little forwards the feeling of security when they gamble for steals and it enables us to go into the full-court press if the opportunity presents itself.

With our big man back, we tell our other players to get back quickly and square off with their *shoulders parallel to the base line.* That puts them *in front* of the opposition, not beside them. If they get caught behind, however, it is their duty to "go for the ballhandler," stop his advance, worry him, slap the ball away, swamp him to prevent a pass-off. The extra pressure often slows the advance of the ball, sometimes drives the ballhandler to a side line or into ball-protection positions where a double-team may take place.

Also on our offensive foul shot set-up, we assume that our opponents will take possession of the rebound angles where they are standing, so we put little pressure on them for those spots. Instead we have our tall rebounders step for the middle of the lane and reach for the tip over the outstretched hands of the defense and in front of the defense. We play only one man back—our tallest player—so we use our men (other than the two strong rebounders) to "trick" the opposition. On one set-up we'll have a third man on the foul line contesting for a spot against their third man set in front of our foul shooter to form their defensive rebound triangle. When he plays there, our foul shooter doesn't go for the rebound, but slides off to cover an area on the press.

On the next foul shot, however, we may have that man playing behind a big rebounder right under the goal. From this spot he's supposed to slide between the rebounder and the base line as the two big boys fight each other. Sometimes our "wild card" player gets an easy crip if the contest between the big men is extra tough.

10

Fifteen Simple Warm-Up Drills for the Patterned Fast Break

No drill is worth a hill of beans of it isn't run properly. A drill isn't worth anything either, if it has no lesson to teach. Therefore, we select our drills carefully in order to teach a phase of the game we intend to play; then we demand that the drills be executed properly. If a player runs through drills lackadaisically, making bad pass after bad pass, we immediately call his attention to his errors. Sometimes we find our whole squad begins to run a drill like a group of sleepwalkers. When that happens we stop, call everybody's attention to the fact, get down into position and start all over again. We've found that players often "stand too high" to play ball properly. We tell them to get down, get their knees bent (not their backs) and "get their noses behind the ball," their hands up in front of their noses; on their passes, they must put the ball in the next man's hands. When they do that and we all explode at the right moments, the drills look good. We're doing what we set out to do.

We've also found that the coach must be "on top of the play" as his players run the drills. If he's over in the corner talking to a fan or a father, his players suffer. We've found it's better to start the drills on a whistle and demand that all players be on the court when the drills begin. Sometimes we lock the doors so nobody can bother us. Friends of players hanging around often divert the attention of key men. Locked doors keep that from happening. Also, locked doors keep players from being late. If they understand you won't open the door for them if they're late, they get to practice on time or they call to explain why they will be late.

After warning a player who continues to make mistakes in his passes and shots during drills, he is punished by making him run a lap or two right then. Nobody waits on him—he just goes—at top speed. If he continues in his errors, we send him home for the day, give him a ball and tell him to practice on his own during the evening; to return the ball in the morning. He may not practice, but again he might. Even if he doesn't, then carrying the ball home and back has a stigma to it. The player will work a little harder next time. He doesn't want to be bothered with the ball again.

After the first day or so of getting acquainted with the drills, the players should have little trouble with them; however, we've found a coach has to explain again and again just what he's trying to teach the players with a certain drill. Often one player won't be paying any attention; even when he says "Yes, Sir, Coach"— after you explain it to him.

For instance, we've had our most trouble in recent years getting players to "widen out" on the fast break. Many of them want to get down the court *before* the ball, so they get into the habit of running up and down the middle of the court near the ballhandler. Many of them actually race up and down the court a step or so *behind* the ballhandler and don't even know what they are doing. We have to stop them again and again to explain that the first move is not down the court but to *widen out* and "grab a lane." Some don't even know what a "fast-break lane" is.

We emphasize again, the coach must do his hardest work

with his drills. It's here that team play is developed. The coach must be on top of the play all the time to see that what he is trying to teach is learned.

Take, for instance, the fast break: The coach must be on one end to see that the rebound and the outlet passes are made properly. He must also be at the other end of the court to see that the drive for the basket is made with proper effort. A fast break that is ended by some lazy player loafing through a gliding crip shot teaches nothing. Thus, the coach, unless he is unusually fast, can't toss the ball up for the rebound, then be on the other end to see that a player "drives *through* the plane of the basket." He must either station himself at midcourt or he must be on one end and his assistant on the other. *Both ends* of the fast break must be taught properly.

After a coach has selected his drills for teaching purposes he must be careful to see that his players don't get tired of running them. There is a "point of saturation" somewhere that he must strive to reach. He wants his players to be perfect, but he doesn't want them overworked—neither does he want them underworked. A good coach will know that point; it doesn't rest with him personally. He must put himself in his players' shoes, look at the situation from their point of view, then eloquently convince them of the importance of the situation. If he convinces them of that importance, then he'll have little trouble teaching them what he wants taught. They'll go along with him.

Here are the drills we use each day. We get tired of some of them ourselves sometimes, but we look to see if *the players* are tired. If they are, we toughen up on our drills, run them hard and fast, then send them home early. We caution here, however: Players can be mentally tired and physically underworked. We always strive to keep them mentally alert and physically well-trained. That's all any coach can do.

Guard-Around Drill

Our guard-around drill teaches our basic half court pattern. This is a drill we picked up from Kentucky many years ago

(Diagram 10-1). It suits our purpose for a drill that hits the forward, then splits the post with the guard breaking down the sideline and by the back door to the basket.

We usually cut our guard straight through the middle on our regular half court setup, but for practice purposes this is a drill all the boys like; in fact, it's a "continuity" we use for pre-game warm-up purposes (Diagram 10-2). It combines ballhandling with

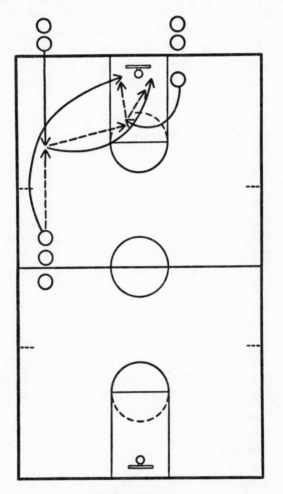

DIAGRAM 10–1

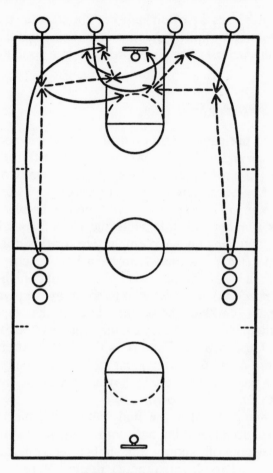

DIAGRAM 10–2

cutting. We like it. We line up three lines—one under the basket, another in the corners and another at the center court sideline. The man at the center starts the play, hits the corner man, and cuts behind him to the basket. The corner hits the pivot cutting acrosss the foul lane and cuts across behind him to split the post. The pivot gives the ball to the first cutter or, as the drill progresses, alternates his passes to one or the other. Then he cuts behind the man he passes to, straight for the hoop. Also, as the drill progresses we often have our shooters lay the ball up on the backboards for tips by the men coming in from the other side or down the middle. The lines progress in a counter-clockwise direction.

Pre-Game Warm-Up Drill

For our pre-game warm-up drill, we use selected pivot men in the corner and under the basket lines; do not alternate them. The other players line up at the center. We use two balls, have two sets of pivots and two sets of cutters on opposite ends of the center line as in Diagram 10-2. We time our breaks so that one "team" is running the drill while the other is passing the ball back to the starting line. We emphasize for this drill four kinds of passes: (1) a push pass (can be a bounce pass) to hit the forward; (2) a backhand pass to feed the pivot (which also can be a bounce pass); (3) an underhand hand-off by the pivot; and (4) a baseball pass (can be a hook pass) back to the center line. We often let the players get fancy on these passes (they like to show off a bit). Our only requirement is that if they attempt a fancy pass in a pre-game drill, they must make it. The ball must end up in the pass receiver's hands. If they can't make it, then don't try it in front of a paying crowd.

In running this drill we find there is a definite danger of ending up shooting nothing but jump shots, so toward the end of the drill we hand off, shoot jump shots after a quick dribble, and have the other two players practice tipping. Here, we emphasize that each player must *jump* and touch the rim, even if he has no chance of tipping the ball. He just sees how high he can jump—first, fingertips on the rim, then palm of hands, then elbow if possible.

In all our drills we like to use as many basketballs as possible. We do not like to have our players standing around whistling at each other and calling encouraging things to each other to build up pep. We want them busy doing things themselves, and doing them efficiently. That builds up personal pride and spirit better than encouraging words.

Ball-Moving Drill

So we use several balls when possible. And we use several balls for the next drill shown in Diagram 10-3. We use two balls, sometimes three. The purpose of this drill is to "keep the ball moving." We want no hesitation at all. The ball must literally glide from hand to hand with no lost motion. There must be no "drawing back," no hesitation. The ball must move on, from

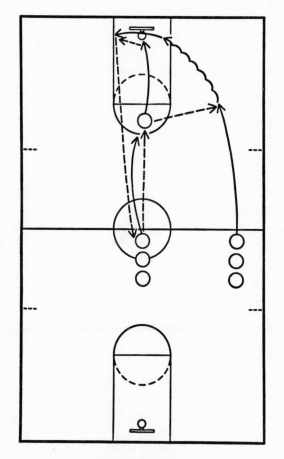

DIAGRAM 10–3

where it's caught. In this drill, you can't "keep yelling" at one player who can't move the ball rapidly. You have to stop and show him what you want; by doing that you're also demonstrating for the other players. Then they begin to take pride in the moves and everybody becomes alert. It's a pretty drill to watch, but the coach has to be alert. This drill can "drag" too, if the coach is dragging.

This drill teaches several styles of passing: (1) feed the pivot, (2) pivot hand-off, (3) rebound pass out, and (4) one hand pass back to center line.

Ball-Moving Variation Drill

With Diagram 10-4 we change the drill a little, feed to the side cutter quicker, have him dribble toward the center, reverse pivot or dribble between his legs to change directions, then drive for the hoop.

Screen-Roll Drill

Diagram 10-5 shows the use of the screen combined with the inside roll on the switch. Every modern player must do this automatically today, so we practice this drill constantly for timing and quick, explosive movements.

Number 1 passes the ball to number 2, and cuts across in front of him and sets up a "moving" screen as the dribbler starts a move towards the basket. The defensive man must do one of two things: (1) he must fight his way through, or (2) the two defensive men switch. If the defense fights his way over the top (1), the screener quickly comes behind the dribbler for a pass. The switch then becomes a *must*. When this happens, the man inside steps *wide* first, then cuts for the basket. By going wide he forces the 2-on-1 situation we desire. If the defense switches, (2) the post man steps wide, hooks his defensive man with a thigh and hip, cuts straight for the basket.

We stress balance on this drill, quick hands and passes made close to the defensive players' bodies so they can't deflect

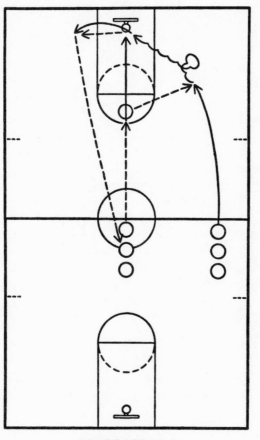

DIAGRAM 10-4

the ball with a waving hand. Sometimes we emphasize a
half-fake, then a pass so close to the defensive player's head that
the ball "parts his hair".

Weave Drills

Diagram 10-6 shows our weave drill. We use this "pass and
screen" drill both on the half court and the full court. If the
pattern is started in the back court, we direct the dribbler to keep

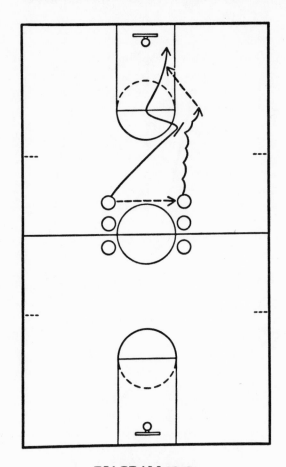

DIAGRAM 10-5

forcing his way forward with his elbow and shoulder until he's actually stopped by the defense. Only then must he cut his dribble, snap pass the ball to the next man and go set up a screen for him. The quick, rocker motion dribble continues until an opportunity for a quick slash at the basket presents itself. We emphasize the *dribbles must* be made quickly without wasting time changing directions or dribbling in one place. Too much dribbling takes the tone off the attack. We also emphasize the fact that the dribbler must not approach the next man too closely before he gives him the ball. There's too much danger in a "hand

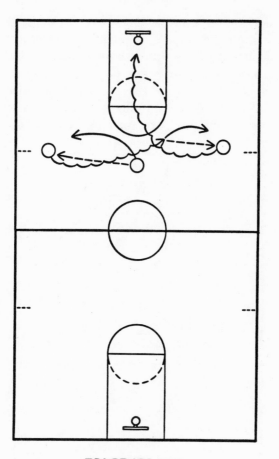

DIAGRAM 10-6

off" of a double-team taking place. We have our players drive to get open, *then* snap the ball to the next man, *then* go and screen him.

Full-Court Dribble Drill

Diagram 10-7 illustrates our dribble drill on the full court. We set a defensive man three feet in front of the man with the ball. On a given signal the dribbler starts his drive toward the right side court until the defense pins him against the sideline.

He then changes direction and goes at an angle until pinned against the other sideline. The move is repeated against the opposite side and, after the third advance, the dribbler is free and in position to drive for the hoop. On the next time around the defense the offense change places. Then for the next time around we allow the defense (with the understanding that they keep perfect balance and keep their bodies between their man

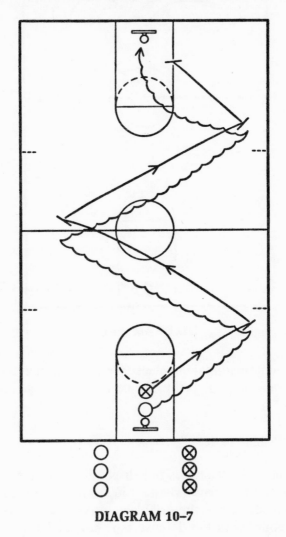

DIAGRAM 10-7

and the basket) to use their hands to disturb the dribbler, attempt to slap the ball away. In doing so they must always remember to drive the dribbler to the sideline, and pin him there while attempting the steal. Then we tell the dribbler to go all the way to the hoop any time the defense lets him; to *make* the defense stop him; never to assume he can't drive just because the defense is standing there. If he can *get his shoulders in front of his man*, then he should go all the way.

Figure "8" Drill

A drill that is easy to run, has both movement and ball-handling is the "figure 8" drill (Diagram 10-8). We use it both on the half court and the full court. We run it from a "half crouched" position (players with "noses behind the ball") and every pass is a quick snap pass. We alert the players with a call then slap our hands together to begin the drill. We use only *two passes*, then the layup. We want to (1) move the ball quickly and (2) go for the boards. The two players, other than the shooter, lunge for the rebound. The one that gets it, quickly turns with his right hand back (or left, if he is left handed), and hooks the ball to the next man in the center line to start the drill again. We emphasize *there must be no drawing back or wasted motion* and we also emphasize that *all three players* go for the boards for tip-in's or rebounds. We make them all touch the rim whether the ball goes in or not. That alerts them for jumping at all times. If the coach isn't careful to do this, one of the players will cut only half way to the hoop before he turns back to the next line. The way he runs the drill is the way he will play the game.

Footwork and Balance Drill

Diagram 10-9 illustrates our footwork and balance drill. It emphasizes a backhand pass and pivoting on the balls of the feet. Two players line up on either side of the foul line. A single pivot man is in the foul circle. Two balls are used. Timing is important. The first man snaps the ball to the second on his side, the second man moves forward and sets up a screen for the first,

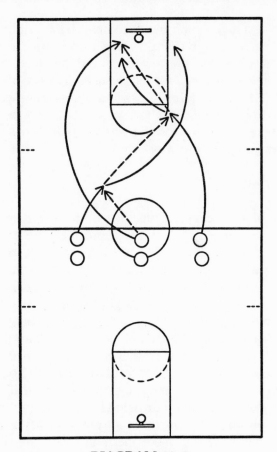

DIAGRAM 10–8

flips the ball back to him. The first man then reverse pivots, bounces a pass to the pivot man and cuts for the basket at the same time. The screener reverse pivots and cuts opposite, by the pivot man for the basket. The pivot gives to either, and walks to the other sideline, where the same process takes place on the other side.

This drill keeps the players close to the floor, well balanced and alert, with every muscle under control. It keeps players from getting their feet mixed up. They have to use the swing of their

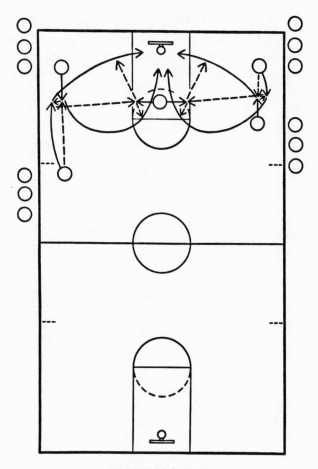

DIAGRAM 10-9

arms and quick, short steps to get started. All the motion is towards the basket. The pivot also learns quick hand-offs.

Globetrotter Drill

Diagram 10-10 is our "Globetrotter" ballhandling drill. We do this for fun, often to a record playing "Sweet Georgia Brown". It's corny and really just a copy of the Harlem

Globetrotters' "fun" warm-up, but the boys like it and it shows off their ballhandling ability. We do this briefly at the end of our pre-game warm-ups. It is really useful, it gets the "ham" out of their system so they won't be tempted to grandstand during the regular game. Players often work long hours on an extremely difficult trick to show off in this drill.

We line the players up in a pair of "threesomes" with our middle men in high post positions, the other two stationed on the sidelines. Each person does his tricks, passes to the next man, until all three have done their drills twice. Then one pivot man

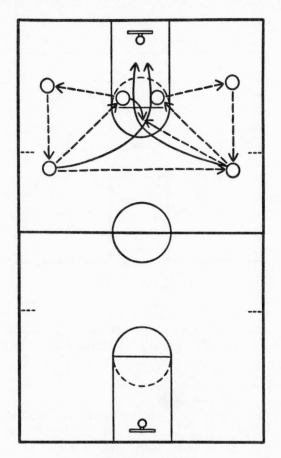

DIAGRAM 10–10

moves to one side with one ball. The other pivot man moves to the middle. The two outside men then pass the ball, one to the other and split the post. The corner men then move outside and the process is repeated. The other pivot man handles the ball on the split-the-post. As the last two men make their last moves, the pivot man dribbles in and dunks the ball, signaling the end of the drill. This drill also allows the pivot men to show their abilities. Before "dunking" was considered "unsportsmanlike," we used to have everybody try to get above the hoop for a dunk. Fans loved it and we sometimes still allow it if the officials are indulgent. However, we've found that coaches of teams who don't have players who can get up that high often are the first to protest, so we're careful who we dunk against.

Jump Shot Drill

Our three-line jump shot drill (Diagram 10-11) is very important to us, so we practice it constantly using two balls in each line. We want a lot of shooting and passing with other players moving around on the court. We mark off three spots on the court, and take all our jump shots from one of these three positions. These are the spots we use on our fast break for our jumps. The two spots on the sides are one yard out on the foul line extended; the center spot is exactly where the players stand for their foul shots. We line our players up near the center line, and have them dribble into jump shot position to get the exact movements they will use during the game. We keep the players in the same lines until everybody moves in a counter-clockwise direction at a toot of a whistle. We often make this competitive by playing a game of "21"—a long shot counts two; crip shots, one.

We again emphasize the importance of this jump shot which has all players shooting *facing* the basket. This is especially important for the big centers. They must be able to score from these spots so the defense can't sag off of them.

We also emphasize the arm and wrist motion on this shot. We want the ball released at the top of the jump with the full body motion behind it. We want our players to stretch the arms

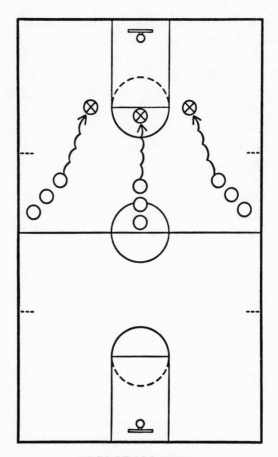

DIAGRAM 10–11

far up in the air for the release. They don't necessarily have to leap high. We've had some very good players who actually released the ball from *behind* their heads. We never tried to stop them.

Speed Dribbling Drill

Diagram 10-12 shows a dribble drill we use to teach speed dribbling. It also teaches the defense to *get ahead* of the dribbler and to "*Square Off*" to keep the dribbler from going all the way to the hoop. It also helps get our players in shape, since it is very strenuous.

We give the dribbler a one-step start on his man and, on a given signal, the race begins. The defensive man must get all the way in front of his man before he squares off. He must not attempt to slap the ball away unless his man beats him to the area of the offensive foul circle. He must not foul his man. This

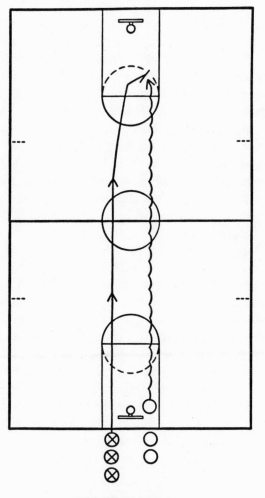

DIAGRAM 10–12

does away with a "lazy" defense that merely slaps at the ball, then gives up. We have our dribblers use the same "speed dribble" the pros are using so successfully at the present time. It's a high dribble that is allowed to bounce as high as the dribbler's face, then pushed ahead and speeded up on the way down. The footwork is fast, with short steps like a sprinter. If a defensive man fouls as he attempts to guard or lets his man shoot unmolestedly, we make him run again against the next man.

As a last desperate move by the defense, we allow him to pin the ball against the board or goal tend. We know this is a rather dangerous process. Players like to do this; they'll often let their men by and then run for the "pin position." They leap for the basket to deflect the ball because everybody "oooh's" and "aaah's" when he's successful. We do not like to see him give away a good position for a bad one, much in the manner of a little guard who actually lets his man by him in order to try for a steal on his dribble. We don't believe in giving up a good defensive position for a gamble. We merely tell our players to do everything possible to prevent the ball from going in the hoop, even to goal tending. If the ball is going in anyway, we'd rather have a goal tending call made than just to give the opposition two points. A team that goal tends all the time has more prestige than one who can't get up that high.

In one game we had last winter, the first ten points the opposition made was on goal tending calls. Fans went away talking about how high our players could jump. Too, goal tending is good psychologically—the offense begins to look for the defensive play. It sometimes breaks up the rhythm of their play. One blocked shot and fast break the other way can sometimes turn the tide that is beginning to run against a team. It gives them a lift; they like to do it, so that's why we encourage them. It costs us nothing. A goal tending call results in two points; so does a successful basket, so let your players goal tend. Officials, even the best ones, may not call everything "goal tending."

Run the Lines Drill

"Sprinting the cross lines" (Diagram 10-13) is a must with us at the end of every practice. "Run the lines" means starting with players lined up on one line at the end of the court and sprinting to the foul line (extended), touching the floor with the

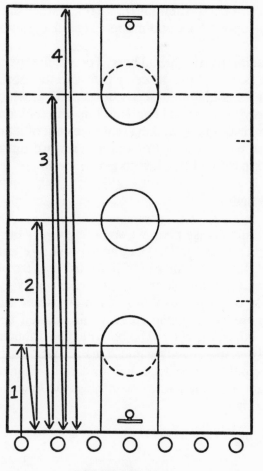

DIAGRAM 10-13

fingertips, sprinting back to the start, touching the floor, sprinting without hesitation to the middle line, then back; to the other foul line extended, back; to the end line and back.

We especially like this drill. It's exactly the moves players will have to make during the game. Touching the floor makes them play with knees bent. One reason we always run this drill last is that everybody gets to expend some energy. Some players may have been neglected during practice. They feel overlooked. You can pay special attention to them at this time. It helps everybody keep in shape, no matter what else they've done all evening.

The coach must be careful here. Too much repetition of this will become boring. After three or four sprints, stop. However, if the coach feels his team needs conditioning, which he must force on everybody, he can continue this drill a bit and keep the players from dragging by making real races out of it and allowing the winner of each heat to drop out as a reward for good effort. They'll work hard and run fast to get to stop.

Donkey Ball Drill

For fun and amusement, we sometimes vary our drills with a game of "Donkey Ball" (Diagram 10-14). We get the same effort out of this we would out of hard drills where players race from one end of the floor to the other carrying someone piggy-back in order to develop good leg muscles. But this way it's much more fun. Twenty players are paired up, one as a donkey, the other, the rider. The ball must be dribbled and shots taken exactly as in a regular game. This activity is strenuous, so the coach should see that donkey and rider change positions frequently and that the game doesn't last too long. This contest is very relaxing.

"Pair Up" Drills

Diagrams 10-15 and 10-16 illustrate our "pair up" drills. We use these to get the players to "know each other" better. That

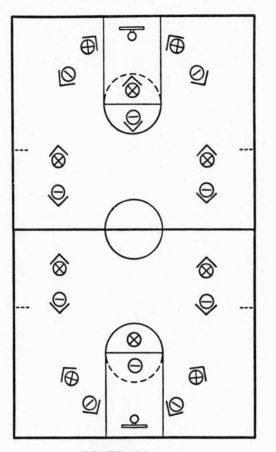

DIAGRAM 10-14

means, to get a better understanding of the "timing" of certain players. Some move faster than others, so the passes to them must be speeded up or slowed down. Passes must be higher to some than to the others. "Teaming up" enables us to gauge those individual characteristics better. We use four lines of players, two lines on either side of the court. We use the half court only for this drill. It is often best to place the forwards and centers in the corners and the back court men outside so they will be working somewhat in their regular game positions as forwards and guards.

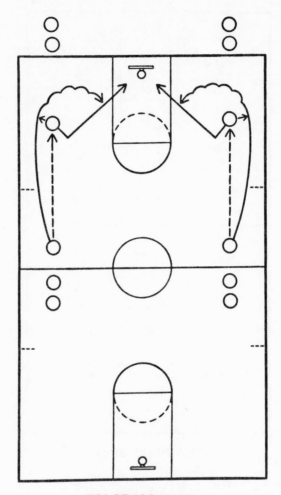

DIAGRAM 10–15

We have a set number of moves we make. These can be varied from day to day. We usually start off with (1) handoffs and rolls to the basket with a dribble, then return passes; (2) pass to forward, dribble across the middle and pass for layup; (3) fake opposite and drive behind a screen, the same way as the original cutter; (4) hit the corner post and cut down the middle, (5) pass, hand off, quick return pass on the roll; (6) pass to forward, fake,

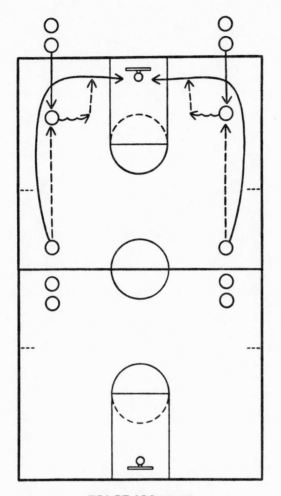

DIAGRAM 10–16

bounce ball between legs to cutter behind ballhandler; (7) pass to forward who drives across middle to basket, flips ball behind him to cutter for layup; (8) pass to forward who returns ball to cutter who dribbles in, flips pass behind him to forward who uses his teammate as screen to drive either side; (9) pass, dribble across middle, lay ball on board for tip-in.

11

Twenty Competitive Drills for Teaching the Patterned Fast Break

Once we didn't think this way, but today we're firm believers in "competitive" practices. Some time ago we lined up a whole series of drills that have competition in them. Now that's all we use. Once upon a time our practices consisted of long hours of routine drills. Sometimes they were very boring. We forced them on our players like medicine, told them they had to do them—"pay the price" if they were going to be great ballplayers. Now we believe the players and coaches, too, enjoy the practices almost as much as they do games. In them, we've found variety and freshness.

We have to repeat the same things often in our drills; we have to make some moves so many times they become routine in order to achieve consistency in perfection. We know consistency takes drills for long hours without end, so we strive each day to give our drills infinite variety. We do the same things but we do them in different ways.

A few years ago when we came onto the court for practice we often observed that the players liked to pair up, play one-on-one or two-on-two games. We immediately put a stop to such "foolishness." Every good coach knew pick-up games meant waste of time, something players did only when the coach wasn't looking. We preferred that our players take long shots and follow them with crips. That we did religiously and formally each day for at least thirty minutes of the practice. We gave each player a ball, told him to follow up his own shots for rebounds so he would learn to go for the ball in the game. We still do this each day, but we don't do it at the first of every practice. Now we go straight into drills. We get the same things done without wasting so much time. If we ever shoot jump shots or outside shots, we have a big boy under the basket, rebounding and tossing the ball out quickly. We want to get a lot of shots off in only a few minutes. We teach our outside shooters to run for a new position, have every muscle poised, feet in the right position ready to release the ball on a good shot, as soon as the rebounder gets the ball back to him and it touches solidly into his hands (no wasted motions).

When we put a stop to that one-on-one play we were working against nature. Now, we've got her on our side—we joined up with her. We let them play. In fact, we encourage it. We tell them to "choose up," get a game going at each basket as soon as they come on the court. Those little "pick-up" games teach everything we want taught, and they do it in "game" situations. It's a natural way to start practices. (Ironically enough, sometimes the players prefer to go it alone; now that it's legal they don't want to do it.)

We let them work for perhaps ten minutes one-on-one, then we join couples to make two-on-two. After a few more minutes we make it three-on-three. As the season progresses we switch partners to gain variety in our practices, but we like to keep our guards together sometimes adding a regular forward to them to begin to get the feel of the team play we expect the varsity to develop.

Quite often we find lone players who wish to work on a

specialty of theirs at the start of practice. We encourage them to do this, providing they are really getting up a sweat. Our only requirement is that they are working and shooting continuously. On top of all our practices it's understood that they'll shoot for at least an hour daily on their own time.

After our "informal" workouts, we go at our formal pre-game warm-up drills in earnest. Those consist of crip shooting and quick passing drills, using as many balls as possible in order to keep all players moving. We believe "warm-up" drills are for "warming up," so we make each drill brief and we use a great variety, changing them constantly as the season progresses. Fans get tired of the same old pre-game drills they saw in December being run the same way the last of March—because we do too, we keep changing our drills. We're still doing the same things but we're doing them in different ways. We're still making our moves automatically even though they're started in a different way.

Once upon a time we practiced our drills for the days we weren't playing on the half court. Now we move them back so we have ³/₄ of the court to run. We believe these wider patterns help develop the full-court ability to run. We never allow our defensive men to retreat to the basket area before they pick their men up. We make them fight all the way back, then toughen up and double-team when we get the team defenses together. It makes for better ball all the way.

In order to make of our drills real *teaching* drills, we found out years ago to watch our players when they were practicing by themselves, making their moves. Then we put a fair defensive man on them, told them to make the same moves, and watched them develop. We then put defensive men with quick hands on them, those good defensive men who play solid defense *with hands near the ball* at all times, making quick stabs at the ball as they retreated or advanced. We then found out how expert our players were. We picked those who could go the best, on the best defense, for our first string. A coach must remember it isn't just "moves" that count. It's *moves on good defense that enable the player to put the ball in the hoop*. Moves don't count unless the player can shoot. The ball has to go into the hoop for the player to really be good.

Here are the patterns we use in our daily practices. Every one has a purpose that fits in with our style of play, or we wouldn't run it. And too—all our drills put together teach everything we want taught.

When we go into our daily routines, we plan each day carefully. We study what we're weak at, what we need to work on, select the drills, set the time to be spent and then draw up our schedule. We try to hold each workout to two hours, but we don't really worry about it. If, at the end of our regular drills, we think we still need a full-game scrimmage, that is what we do. If we think we need another workout, we sometimes plan two for the next day.

In other words, we don't put any limits on our possibilities, but we do hope to be reasonable, remembering that high school athletes play for fun. It's a fact, too, that those same athletes love hard work, want to perfect themselves. They are proudest when you work them the hardest. They brag about tough workouts—they love the real challenge.

When we start our daily practices, we start slowly, then get tougher. We vary our practices from the full court to the half court and back. When we rest, we shoot foul shots. We keep everybody busy every moment of the practice.

Some drills are so important we want an assistant coach on one end of the floor, the head coach on the other. We want every drill run to perfection—all the way. Practicing the wrong way, creates bad habits.

Dribbling-the-Lines Drill

Our first drill is an easy one. We practice this to be sure that everybody is able to dribble the ball without any trouble at all, and without having to look at the ball. If any of our players are weak at dribbling, we send them down to the "B" ream to learn. We call this drill "dribbling the lines" (Diagram 11-1). For this drill we place defensive men in the center of the jump circle, and have them go after the ball (only in the circle) as the dribblers pass them. That enables the ballhandlers to spin, slide, pivot, hook, yet continue to advance the ball as they are supposed to. Too often we see players trying to operate against a press do it in a defensive manner. We want our players to *attack* a press hungrily every time they see one. We want them to glory in the challenge, fling a tough forearm and wrist out in front of them, and beat the pesky presser away from the ball.

The player starts his dribble in the right corner, slides along

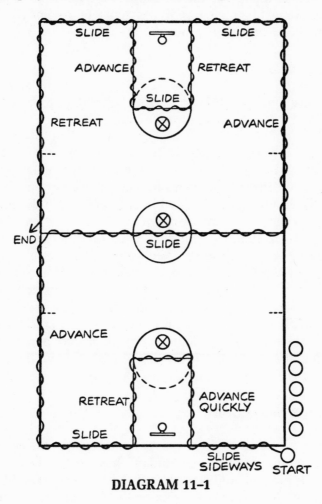

DIAGRAM 11-1

the lines parallel with the end line, advances up the court on the foul lane, across the center of the foul circle protecting the ball—retreat back to the end, then to the corner. A quick dribble takes him to the middle of the court where he starts his slide sideways to the opposite sideline where he advances to the end line, across, back down the foul lane, across, up to the end line, across, then back to the center line. He has completed the dribble. Three men have annoyed him at the center of each jump circle. This must be done rapidly, each player starting as soon as the man ahead of him has touched the first foul lane.

Top Speed Drill

Two or three repetitions of this are enough. These can be done in a minute or so. By watching, a coach can find out his dribblers in a hurry. There's no "covering up" in the drill. You can either do it or you can't. No need wasting time with those who can't dribble. After a few moments of dribbling, we go to another drill. This drill (Diagram 11-2) is also for ballhandling, especially dribbling, but it also teaches a bit about defense. We have our dribblers advancing down the floor *at top speed* against defensive men *standing still* near the foul shot line extended. The defense can do whatever they want to. They soon learn how fast a man with a full head of steam up can go around a defensive man who doesn't retreat and "get into step" with the offensive player. We have the drivers take one shot, then get out of the way. If we were using only one fast-break lane, we'd fight for the rebound, but two more lines of players are coming in right after the first one. However, be sure to have the defense stick with their man all the way to the basket.

Long-Pass Rebound Drill

Next we begin to form our pattern for the fast break. We begin it, of course, with a rebound off the boards (Diagram 11-3). We set our big man under the boards with a defensive player on his back. We give him the inside position, make him "hold" his

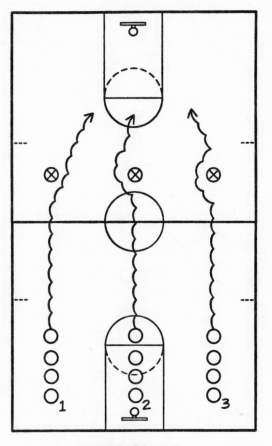

DIAGRAM 11–2

man on his back by putting his hands out back of his hips and turned back, feeling for his man. He is not to let his man get around him, and he is to rebound so as to reach the ball at the height of his leap, with arms completely outstretched. He reaches even a bit higher with one hand, "snatches" the ball out of the air, then he comes down twisting the ball behind him and begins his outlet pass. This pass can be whatever is necessary, a hook or a plain baseball pass, but it must be quick and it must have some "zip" to it. Sometimes our players come down "stiff

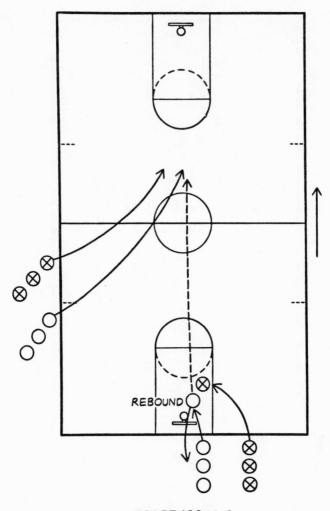

DIAGRAM 11–3

legged," get the ball out with a two-handed pass from back of the head; sometimes they even flip it out while still in the air. That's hard to do on this setup, however, since he must usually pass the ball half the length of the court. We make this pass long on purpose, to get the rebounder used to throwing long, *quick* passes that are easy to handle. We don't want *hard, heavy* passes that stiffen up the wrists of the receiver. We want the ball to get to the driver in a hurry, and we want him able to do something with the ball when he gets it.

We also place a defensive man behind the forward cutting to receive the pass. He *starts behind* the offensive cutter—away from the ball. The forward must time his move and make the angle of his cut such that the defensive player is unable to move in and intercept the pass. If the defense gambles and misses the interception, the forward has a wide-open crip shot. If the defense stays back, then we have the two players operating quickly and at top speed on the one-on-one situation.

We stress that the forward *must not allow himself to be driven away from the basket.* He must *get his shoulders by his man,* then *continue on* to the basket and get off a good shot that can't be blocked. The defensive man must play properly. He cannot "roughhouse" or foul his man. If he does not choose to gamble, he retreats in a proper manner with his feet, arms and shoulders between his man and the basket. He watches what the offense is trying to do, keeps him away from the basket, hopes to force him into a bad or a poor percentage shot (he uses his wrists and forearm to do this). He does not allow the dribbler to "shove" him along. Then he blocks *his man out, first,* and goes for the rebound. If he is unable to keep his man away from the backboards, he goes right along with him, all the way to the boards. He waits *for the driver to gather himself together* for the layup. Then, *watching the ball,* not the man; and trying *not to anticipate* the move, he quickly slaps exactly where the offense wishes to put the ball up. If his timing is right, he'll "cap the ball." Often he can "come out running" with it. A pin against the boards is also legal, providing the defense can pin the ball on the way up, before it begins its downward flight. We work on that, too.

Three-Man Snap-Pass Rebound Drill

As soon as our rebounders begin to tire of the long pass we begin our "three-man, rebound, snap-pass drill" (Diagram 11-4) on the half court. Nobody has to run much here. We place one line at the outlet pass spot on the right side of the court, another

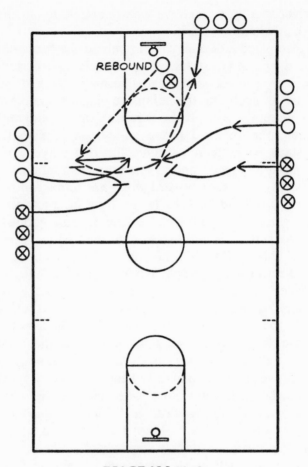

DIAGRAM 11-4

on the left, a third under the boards. We place defensive lines with them "on their backs." The rebounder moves into position, and the first two "forwards" move into regular "defensive" positions near the "dotted lines" of the foul circles facing the basket. Their defensive men drop off near them. The rebounder gets his man on his back and the coach tosses the ball on the board so it will come off on the side he wants it to for the proper pass-out in the direction he's set up for. The ball is then passed to the outlet spot, then snapped across to the second forward, then to the next rebounder getting ready. He hands it to the coach. The offense rotates in a counter-clockwise motion, then they move in on defense. The defensive men also rotate counter-clockwise, then move in on the offense.

We use two balls to keep things moving. If a ball is intercepted, the players quickly get out of the way and move to the next position. This pattern teaches the players to "prevent" interceptions by pressure defenses, and still go on to the offense in spite of it. Our philosophy is *go directly at the defense.* Don't wait on it or dodge it, make it commit itself at once.

Half-Court Three-Lane Drill

The basic fast-break pattern in all usual systems ends up with the middle man handling the ball in the middle lane of the court and two other players occupying the side lanes. We use the drill shown in Diagram 11-5 to teach the proper manner of approaching the goal on a 3-on-2 or 3-on-1 situation. This drill is run on the half court and can be used to "rest" the players a bit after strenuous runs on the full court. Play starts just back of the center line with snap-passes between the three lanes. Then the players move out with the center man dribbling in and forcing the defense into their planned set up. If the top defensive man doesn't come out and pick the dribbler up, he merely shoots an easy jump shot. The side men quickly move in, get inside positions, back up a couple of steps and go for the boards. We emphasize here that if the side men go straight in as they would on their driving angles, they will be too far under and out of the play on rebounds. They must quickly get *in front of the boards* and back up a bit. Then they can take one step and leap higher for the rebound.

If the top defensive man comes out half heartedly with one foot extended, we have our center man, who is always an excellent dribbler, fake at slowing down, quickly make his move to get his shoulders by this first defensive man, then go to work on the second who usually charges in also. A good sharp pass at

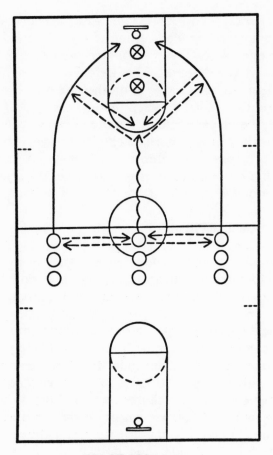

DIAGRAM 11-5

the right moment to the right spot will have a side man laying the ball right in the basket.

If the two defensive men play it properly and stop the center man, cover the first pass, retreat back for the second, with arms flailing, then we begin our usual "triangle" passing pattern. We attempt to move the ball faster than the defense can move, handling the ball on fingertips and moving in behind the defense to get position while they are shifting. When we get them "leaning," then a fake and a quick pass in the opposite direction will get a man open.

This must not take much time. Another threesome is waiting. It's a good idea on this drill to line the players up with the ones who are expected to play together in the games to play together in this drill. For instance, we always line up our starting guards with our starting "ballhandling" forward. Then we put our two big post men in with the next best ballhandling guard. We develop good ballhandling combinations this way. This drill often develops the quick, fancy passing we like to brag about; the kind fans love. Players go at it crouched down, hands up near their faces and they "move the ball on," talking to each other as they do it. The defense gets steamed up and the passing must be really good to get an open shot. After a successful attempt with good passes, a ripple of applause often runs through the gymnasium. Players love good passing and fancy movements that are successful.

Full-Court Three-Lane Drill

We use our three-lane passing drill (Diagram 11-6) for several purposes: (1) to teach the players to run at top speed and still be able to handle the ball efficiently; (2) to stay *wide* and in the proper lanes, to time their breaks so they won't get to the passing spots too early; (3) to place the passes where the player can handle them (we never *lead* a man, we hit him where he is and where his hands are); and (4) for conditioning purposes.

This is almost the same as our half-court three-lane drill, with the full-court movement added. We wish our players to run their drills exactly as they will use them in game situations. We start this drill with passes merely for efficiency of administration. Three defensive men have been placed in the jump circles to bother the passers, cause them to walk, double dribble or merely slow them down. We want this drill to teach our offensive players to "charge" the defense, make the defense commit itself, get close to the defensive players before passing

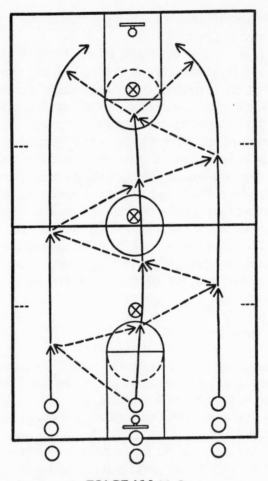

DIAGRAM 11-6

the ball. The approach to the offensive foul lane should be controlled with every player well-balanced and ready. Then, as the ball enters the foul circle, all players should "explode." The big drive should begin here. The "ultimate" effort should be expended at this point. Each player should run the lanes at great speed, yet keep a little energy in reserve so that their drive for the basket has plenty of extra speed and muscle power. The player should not be "gliding" as he makes his shot. He should be *running through the board* with extra effort made at the last moment of release of the ball, instead of floating uncontrolled in the air.

The angles of the drives for the hoop should be different from the fast-break lanes at the end of the court. They should be *exactly the same* as the team practices its crip shots in. Players who are not shooting should be eager for the rebounds. They should be crouched, feet in good contact with the floor, hands up ready to move in any direction for the rebound. The play is never over until the ball goes through the hoop or a defensive player has control of it. If the two defensive players succeed in stopping the first drive, then the "three-on-two" triangle passing pattern begins with the fast passes, then a fake to draw the defense into a lean, a pass by him and a side man slipping in behind the defense to lay the ball in the hoop.

"Grab the Three Lanes" Drill

We also vary this with a "grab the three lanes" drill (Diagram 11-7). We set five players up in defensive positions across the court in the 2-1-2 zone defense pattern with a couple of opposing players near the foul line. The coach dribbles the ball around and simulates a steal or interception at various positions. The off side players anticipating interceptions, grab lanes, begin to sneak away on the fast break patterns *before* the ball is in the hands of a teammate. That enables them to get a jump on the defense. Then lob pass over the defense to the open man results in a quick basket. If a defensive man gets back, then we work the two-on-one. If two men get back, then we work three-on-two. Our basic moves in our fast breaks are (1) to get open down the court and (2) to get the ball to the front man. All our work must be to this end. The ball must move quickly and unselfishly *to the front man.* One unnecessary dribble may kill the move where a quick lob pass at the split second of interception would get the man open.

A second's delay in movement down court by the man who is in the proper position to lead the break can be fatal. Also if he

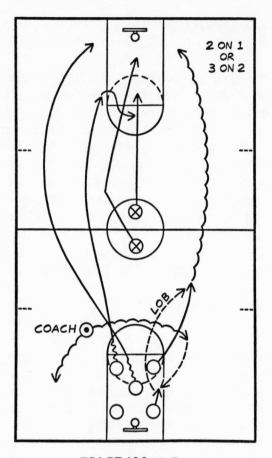

DIAGRAM 11-7

goes a split second too soon, he'll mess things up by drawing the defense with him. This unexplainable, untimeable move must be worked on for long hours. Some players have instincts that tell them how and when to cut in order to get a jump on the defense. Those players seem always to be open. Fans and rival players often remark that they "could shoot crip shots like that," if somebody would feed them the ball all the time like his teammates seem to feed him.

It isn't that simple. Teammates don't often feed one man

unless he has certain abilities to get open. Then they're glad to get him the ball. That's the mark of the All-American ability to pass and get open. The great player makes things look so simple and so easy that it looks as if everybody could play the way he does; however, let the coach substitute another *good* player in his place, and the team just doesn't seem to click as well. Playing with a real All-American is fun. He releases the ball timely—he passes well—he expects quick passes in return. The greatest scorers we have ever had in this area of the country were also the greatest passers.

Those things come by instinct. The ability to turn the ball loose is often all that keeps a good player from being a truly great one. This drill attempts to get the player to move the ball at once, without a quick dribble against the floor. That dribble often "kills" our fast attack.

Two-on-One Half Court Drill

This is a simple drill that has two players moving quickly against one defensive man (Diagrams 11-8 and 11-9). The idea is to get a basket quickly before the defense can get aid from his teammates rushing to help him. Speed in passing is most urgent. You can't wait for someone to make a mistake; you have to *make him* make a mistake.

Often players handling the ball become so used to going to the middle of the court on a fast break that they go to the middle of the court even in a two-on-one situation. That move often enables one defensive man to play a zone defense and guard both of them. Unless a trailer comes along, the offense is stuck and a bad percentage shot is the result.

We have found over the years that it's almost impossible for one defensive player to stop two offensive players on the fast break. The only chance the defense has is to fake, windmill his arms and yell in hopes of worrying the driver, causing a walk or missed shot.

The seasoned offensive player knows this situation, does not relax. In fact, he becomes tense and even more alert as the

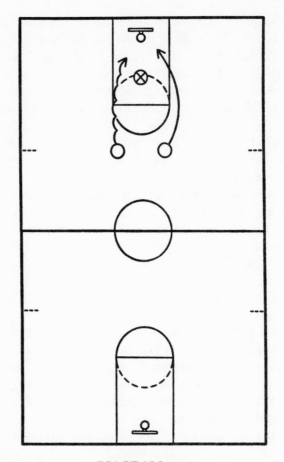

DIAGRAM 11–8

ball gets close to the hoop. He knows he has a problem to solve. He does not relax until the ball is in the hoop. He expends his best effort here.

We teach our offensive players to carry the ball *all the way to the hoop* if the defensive player retreats all the way to the area under the hoop. We emphasize that a good player will keep "threatening" the pass until he has an opening all the way to the basket; then he carries the ball to the hoop. It's the same thing as a base runner in baseball being slowed down by fake passes; the

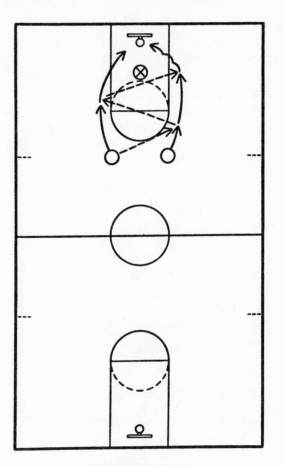

DIAGRAM 11-9

fielder gets close by the threats, then he runs the runner down. The driver threatens to pass, forces the defense to play for the pass, then edges in beside him.

Five-Man Rebound, Pass-Out and Cut Drill

Our five-man rebound, pass-out and cut drill is actually our fast-break pattern set up in drill form. The way we alternate the players is shown in Diagram 11-10. We place three lines under one board and two lines facing them out near the foul circle where the guards usually play on defense. The lines under the basket form the rebound triangle, the two outside lines are the forwards; the groups do not change. The rebounder takes the ball off at one side, passes it out to the ballhandler in proper position on the right or left. He passes it on to the other forward cutting across. The two lines of ballhandlers standing near the middle are supposed to be there bothering the offense.

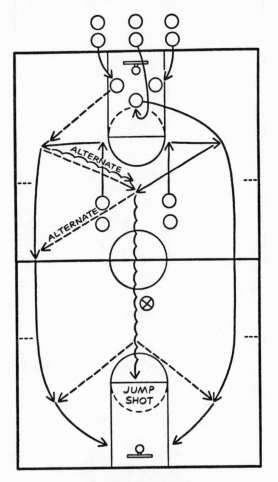

DIAGRAM 11–10

If the second outlet pass cannot be made, the ballhandler merely dribbles to the middle and the middle man cuts on across to the open lane.

Defensive men are often placed in the middle and offensive foul circles to worry the ballhandlers and slow them down, if possible. A smart ballhandler will hit the side cutter facing him, continue on and take a return pass to set up the triangular attempt in front of the basket. We use three or four basketballs for this drill and have managers stationed along one sideline to take passes, returning the ball to the coach who tosses the ball on the board for the rebounds.

Sometimes, to the signal of a whistle, we turn all the waiting ballhandlers in the two lines near the center court loose as defensive players, and have them suddenly attempt to steal the ball by double teams, swamping tactics, or intercepts of passes. This keeps our offensive ballhandlers alert at all times to the danger of sudden pressing tactics. We wish to train our players to quickly go into a "protective," aggressive offense without going into a defensive shell, even for a moment. We want them to be able to whirl, swerve, reverse pivot quickly, still moving the ball forward and looking ahead for the good pass or the good drive that will get us a bucket.

Two-on-One Full-Court Drill

In early-season play we soon discover what shape our ballplayers are in by our two-on-two full-court game. This drill needs no diagram. Two players are merely teaming up against two other players in a full-court game. There's an art to playing this game. Players must be warned not to "drive through" the boards too far, since they will have to get back quickly on defense, and one second of relaxation after a successful shot may mean chasing the opposition down from behind going the other way. The players soon learn to try to outscore the other side if a basket is scored on them, so the ball zips up and down the court at great speed for a little while. Even the best players "run down," and a new foursome must be substituted. The exhausted players are only too ready to collapse on the floor at the sideline. After two or three repeat performances, they will begin to see the need of being in shape to play the game of fast-break basketball.

We have only a few rules for this game. Players go the way they're headed until they score a basket. Then the team that gets the rebound or gets the ball coming through the hoop, takes the offense the other way. Thus a pair of players play defense until they can get the ball by their own efforts, not by rules alternating control of the ball.

Three-on-Three Half-Court Drill

Our next drill rests our players somewhat by having them moving on the half court. The three-on-three screens and roll for the hoop drill (Diagram 11-11) teaches the inside roll as well as any drill we know. Play starts with the middle offensive man in possession of the ball. He starts his dribble, bores in toward the basket (drives all the way if he can), then snaps a pass to the next ballhandler and goes and screens for him. If a switch is made, he steps backward with his inside foot, hooks his man behind him, widens out and goes for the board. If at all possible, the ballhandler makes a quick dribble toward the middle of the court, then hits him for the layup. (This is the same movement we use on our "Carolina four-corner offense", with the exception that we do not screen in the wide pattern. We pass and go for the hoop.) If no pass is apparent, the dribbler then bores in toward the hoop (goes all the way if the defense lets him), and then passes to the next man and sets up a screen for him. The inside roll again takes place. The process is repeated until a goal is scored or the ball is intercepted; then the three offensive men take the defense. The defensive men move to the rear of the line and a new offensive trio begin their drive for the basket.

The best players show their wares in this drill. They must be able to dribble the ball and also to pass it. If their inside roll is too fast or too slow, then they don't get the feed inside. Timing has to be perfect.

Some players we have had run this drill so well we've used

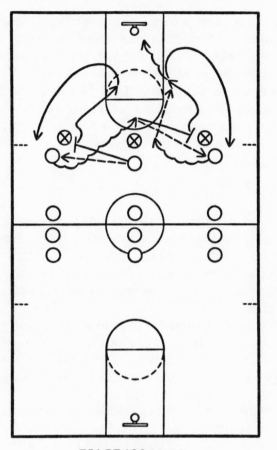

DIAGRAM 11–11

it for our regular offense. It's simple, easy to learn and very effective. Add two wide pivot men to it, and teach them to go for the boards when their defensive men switch off on a driver and the offense is tricky. The court is well balanced and the players are in good position to convert to defense. The only weak point is rebounding. The pivot men, playing wide to leave the driving lanes open, have to move fast to get the rebound positions. Too, a zone defense or a sagging defense will give this pattern a lot of trouble. Against close-to-the-basket defenses, chances of interceptions are high. If a team continues to run them (shooting only crips because of rebound weaknesses) it's likely to begin to play "catch-up" ball. Nobody can win modern games shooting only crips, unless they are playing "possession ball." Fans don't go for slowdown tactics today. They like to see action. Full-court ball gives it to them, so we rarely get into half-court patterns to any degree; but we have to learn these quick, close moves in order to play on the full court.

"Twenty-One" Drill

Sometimes we don't wish too much competition on the defense and we feel we need to practice a little jump shooting. So we line up in three lines (Diagram 11-12), dribble up to the three jump-shot spots, shoot a long one, and follow it up with a crip shot. We add a bit of competition by playing a game of "21". Long shots count two, crips count one. We keep the lines intact for the game, then move them over to another spot. After each group has shot from all these positions, the drill is over.

We use a "passive" defensive man most of the time. He tries to block the shot, then block out his man on the rebound, but he doesn't go for the boards.

If we want to make the drill tough, we line the offense up with a defensive man pressing them from the start of the dribble, going for the boards on rebounds. We time the start of each group so each has the opportunity to play all of the half court, yet still be counting the game of "21".

Race-for-the-Boards Drill

Back on the full court again, we line up three men on the fast break, put three defensive men two steps behind them— race for the boards (Diagram 11-13). The defense has to get in front of the offense and square off. The offense has to pass the ball between lanes and beat the defense down the court. This is sheer speed, straight-away ball. No fakes are allowed; no maneuvers are allowed. If the defense gets in front, then they have won and the ball is brought back for the next players. If one offensive man is able to outrace his defense, then he gets the ball and drives for the hoop. If a defensive man cuts him off, then he must pass to the man left open. This is, again, our real fast break set-to-drill pattern. Sometimes we vary this by placing *two* men near the middle of the court, have them retreat

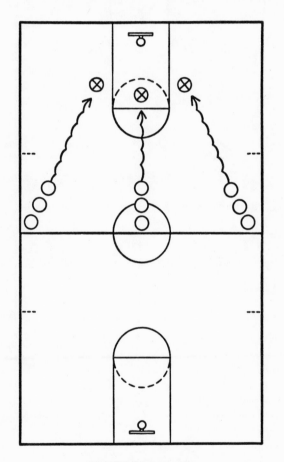

DIAGRAM 11–12

and attempt to cover all three offensive men. This is only a variation of the three-on-two game, but it adds variety to the practice. Sometimes we use this drill one day and the three-on-two another. Rarely do we ever run all these drills on one day, but we do use all of them within the course of a week. We also like to do a lot of scrimmaging. It all takes time.

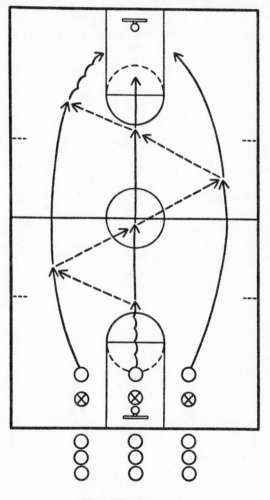

DIAGRAM 11–13

Three-on-Three Game Drill

As the season progresses, we often use our next drill, our "three-on-three game" for fun and conditioning. Again this drill, like the two-on-two drill used earlier in the season is very strenuous, since it is run on the full court. There is no set pattern. It's free-lance all the way, but it's so strenuous the players soon learn not to dribble all over the court. That takes too much energy. They're soon glad to have someone to pass the ball to. Again, the defensive players must get the ball themselves before they can go on offense. We have to substitute a new group often since players run down in a hurry. Sometimes we divide this drill into little rest periods by taking the ball after every goal, throwing the ball up against the boards and letting everybody jump for it. The team that gets the ball goes on offense, the other, defense. This gives the players a second or so to catch a breath. Again, we punctuate this drill by having one team or the other take the ball out of bounds, shoot a foul shot or call a jump ball. These all add variety.

We caution, however, against requiring the defense to play a full-court pressing game. It is better to have the defense pick up all over the court, but not press. There's a difference. Nobody can press all over the court without arranging some switches for team defensive play. That's hard to do with only three men on the defense.

Saturation Drill

As soon as the regular basketball season starts in earnest, we do very little individual work and prefer to use five men together. We want all our drills to be team drills with five men participating. Such a drill is our five-man offense vs. nine-man defense. We've named it our "saturation drill" (Diagram 11-14). We draw lines with a piece of chalk dividing the court into three equal parts. We place three defensive men in each partition. It is their duty to intercept the ball and stop its advance in any way that is legally possible. The offense must rebound the ball off the board and advance it down court with little hesitation. This play takes an alert team to get the ball down quickly. Every offensive man must be used, and the ball must be passed accurately and quickly. No player can go to sleep at any time. This is also a very strenuous game. The offensive players must be changed often. After a score the players turn around and go in the other direction. Everybody should take turns playing offense; however, only the best ballhandlers should be in the key positions to handle the ball under such pressure. If poor ballhandlers are

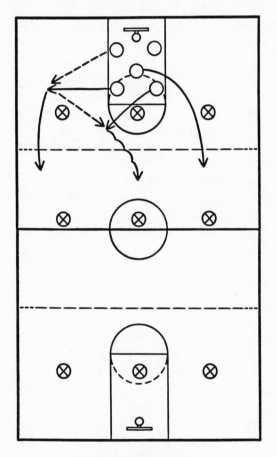

DIAGRAM 11–14

used, then the drill doesn't even get started and the drill disintegrates into chaos; but with quick, sharp actions the drill can sharpen up the best players, the "experts."

Give and Go Drill

One of our best half court drills is our regular "give and go" pattern run in drill fashion (Diagram 11-15). Using this drill gets us well acquainted with all positions. Everybody knows what everybody else is supposed to do. This drill begins with the guard hitting the forward on the right side, and cutting through to the opposite side to grab a good shooting position just outside the foul line. The forward then looks for a pass to the off-side forward who has been screened for a cut to the low pivot position by the center. The center then moves to the high post position again. If the pass into the low post is not possible, the ball is passed back to the standing guard who wheels it across to the center who has the option to shoot or pass to the guard who has cut through. The rotation for the guards is in a clockwise direction. It's really simple. The guard who has cut through steps out of bounds, and returns to the "guard" line. Another guard has taken his place in the "standing" position. On the next play he'll be the cutter. The front line rotates in a counter-clockwise direction—right forward, center, left forward then back to the rear of the line. After running the play to the left side for a while, the offense is changed to the opposite side and the rotation is reversed. To vary this offense the guards have the option of reversing their dribble toward the sidelines at anytime and hitting the pivot. We then run our "split the post" drill which is a simple move, having both guards cutting and the forwards coming out to take their places. The forwards complete the movement by also splitting the post and returning to their previous positions.

Pro-Set Drill

We also run our "pro-set" offense in the same way, with the same rotation. Before the drill is over, we put five defensive men

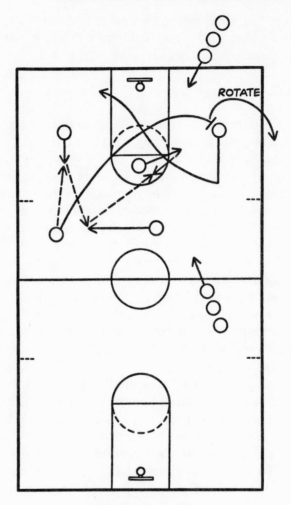

DIAGRAM 11–15

in and operate under game conditions. At this time we do not change positions. We alternate whole teams.

Keep-Away Drill

Diagram 11-16 shows our "keep away" drill. We use this pattern as our "slow down" tactic when we have the game in the bag and want to take only "sure" shots. We tell our players they can shoot only "standing crips" where we are sure of getting the rebounds if we blow the crip. We use a three-man outside, two-in-the-corners setup, always with defensive men on them. The middle ballhandler starts the drill just before the defense attacks. The side ballhandlers stay away from the middle line, play about half way down the sideline of the forecourt, and break out to meet the ball suddenly as the dribbler makes his

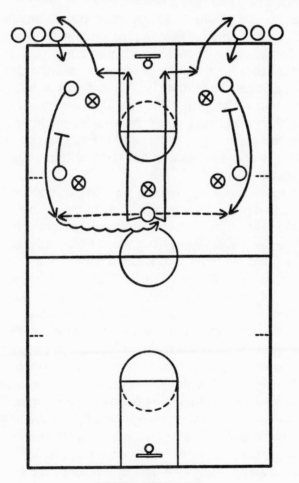

DIAGRAM 11–16

move. The side man must *fake inside* first to draw his defense one step behind him. If the defense refuses to be fooled, the side man drops back into the corner and screens the corner man who breaks out to handle the ball. When he receives the pass, he immediately "freezes" with it, holds his dribble, and freezes his defensive man with him. As soon as the defense starts towards him he starts his dribble, boring in toward the basket. The guard and the forward on the other side make the same maneuvers as the previous two had to get open.

As soon as a player makes his pass to a teammate, he takes one more step, plants his foot in the direction of the pass, pivots off that front foot, and cuts straight for the basket, holding his hand out in front for the pass. If a pass is made to him, the hand is used as a target. The timing is such that, just as he receives the ball, he shoots the crip. We run this drill as a continuity, dropping the corner men out after they've made one complete circuit of the court (right to left and back again, or vice versa). Often we get two new men in at the same time, but that really doesn't matter.

In a game situation, before we start this setup, we make certain all five players know what we are trying to do—whether we want to take shots to keep building up the lead, or we want to swap *time* for ballhandling. We must make sure of what our strategy is, and we must also know what we will do in case the opposition scores. We practice this drill with those things in mind. We often set the clock for two minutes, and tell our ballhandlers they are leading by four points—so set on the ball. In the event the opposition scores a basket on an error by our ballhandlers, however, we must build the score back up to four points before we again set on the ball. Then we turn them loose to run the clock out, calling everything as close as an official would. If, as usually does happen, a defensive man "plays the setup," we teach our players to go straight for the hoop and we hit them for layups. One or two easy crips like this will teach defensive players not to overplay or anticipate.

More than anything else, this drill teaches the value of pass work. If some fancy ballhandler wants to dribble all the way in, we let the corner men sag off on him. The first time he shoots and doesn't get the rebound, we run him a lap around the court for "showboating." If he makes a really good move to get himself open, we compliment him for it.

This "situation scrimmaging" is especially useful near the end of a season. We do this, setting up scores and time remaining on out-of-bounds plays on the sidelines and under the basket.

We also run the keep-away drill to make a team come out of a zone defense. We don't like to "hold the ball" in a stall. We like a lot of action that gets the opposing team upset. Our fans know what we are doing and they enjoy the other team's frustrations. This setup often enables us to build up a good lead before the opposition cools down again.

Tip Ball Setup Drill

Another situation drill is the "tip ball setup" (Diagram 11-17). We line up three lines on one end of the court for rotation. The centers are in the middle line. They (1) play the defensive goal tender, (2) do the tipping, (3) catch the ball after the tip, and swing it bowling style to the first cutter. The forwards and the guards make up the wing men who do the fast breaking; we release the wing man on the right first. He starts the break just *before* the ball is tossed up. We release him early. Sometimes it doesn't hurt for him to get going as the referee moves toward his "toss" position. Anyway, we want him early enough to be past the center line before the tip is well under control of the center receiver. Sometimes that man merely tips the ball on down the court (we let him do that *only if* the defensive men are pressing him on both sides). The second fast-break man cuts in behind this big man in order to scoop up any over-tip. We have our defense set up theoretical situations. Another good situation drill is created by using our out-of-bounds play on the sidelines (Diagrams 11-18 and 11-19). Rotation of the guards is in a clockwise direction. They do not change

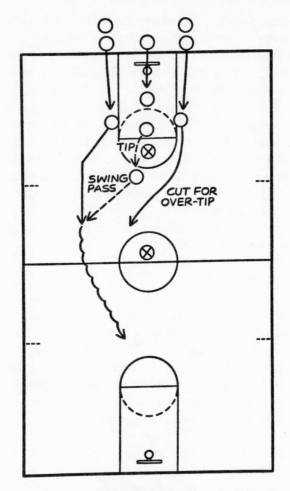

DIAGRAM 11–17

with the front line. Rotation of the forwards is counter-
clockwise. Our continuity is simple. The ball is held over the
head and tossed in to the back guard who catches the ball over
his head and moves it on to the pivot who has moved out one
step and hooked his defensive man behind him. The pivot
quickly swings the ball on an underhand toss to the guard cutting
down the sideline off of a screen by the off side forward. That

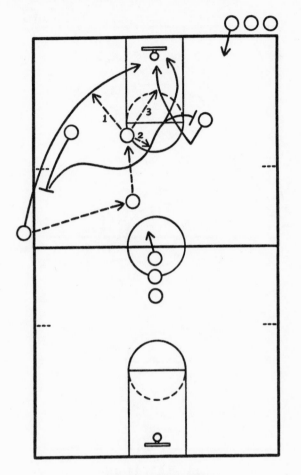

DIAGRAM 11-18

same forward rolls off his screen behind the pivot for an option pass. If he does not get the ball, he continues across the court, and sets up a screen for the off side forward who cuts straight for the basket. The pivot options him. The screener then rolls right in behind his man for another option.

Diagram 11-20 adds the option we use when we can't get the ball to the pivot, or when we are running against a zone defense. The ball swings across the court to the off side forward who

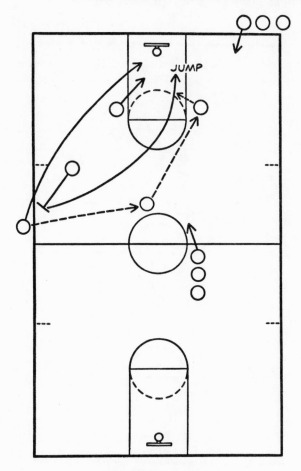

DIAGRAM 11–19

feeds the onside forward cutting off the pivot man. He goes in only to the "second line" of the zone defense where he shoots a jump shot. The pivot and the first cutting guard grab the rebound positions. The rotation is the same. Defense is added whenever the coach wants to, preferably after the drill has been run a few times without it. *Caution:* The coach must sometimes *make* the guard pass the ball into the pivot position. Too often he chickens out at this spot upon the first sign of defensive play. The coach must assure him a pressure defense on the pivot if "unsuccessful" means an easy basket, since the pivot has the option of wheeling and dealing at any time he wants to. A good pressure on the pivot often means the lane to the basket is wide open. All the pivot has to do is to get the ball to the cutter with a little flip pass.

After a few days practice of this drill, we are able to use two balls to keep everybody in motion, with no waiting for the ball to get back to the starting point. Our biggest problem at the start of each season is to get the guards to remember to run the pattern. Often the in-bounds pass is made and the guard freezes onto the ball. He wants to "play with it" a little bit, and we miss a quick basket.

Eleven-Man Continuous Drill

The final drill we will diagram is perhaps our favorite. It can be run continuously for perhaps twenty minutes and the players, and the coaches alike, find it always fascinating. We call it our "eleven-man continuous drill" (Diagram 11-20). If we had to chooose any *one* drill to teach the fast break, this would be it. We line up two defensive players at each end of the court and a player at each of the four "outlet pass" positions. The other players fall in behind those at the outlet pass positions, keeping those spots filled. Three offensive players grab the fast-break lanes and attack the defense on one end of the court. Action continues three-on-two until a basket has been made or someone on defense gets the rebound or makes an interception. Whoever gets the ball goes quickly onto offense, tossing the ball to a player at the outlet pass position. He dribbles down the middle and the three-on-two offense is continued on the other end. This process is repeated endlessly with everybody taking part, running at top speed. Nobody is neglected and the action continues fast and furious.

Sometimes this drill becomes as challenging as a real game. The players loosen up, lengthen their strides and begin to run like greyhounds. That's the patterned fast break we love to run.

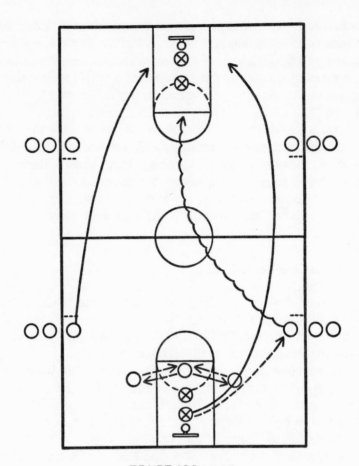

DIAGRAM 11–20

Summary

As we mentioned at the start of this chapter, here are twenty drills we use to teach our fast break. We must warn our readers, however, that no drill is really worth anything unless the coach has something special to teach by it. He must know and emphasize the move he wishes to develop. He must first explain to his players what he is trying to do, what he is trying to correct or what he wishes his players to become expert at. Then he explains how the drill teaches what he wants. We might add here that it would be good also if the coach wishing to teach his team the patterned fast-break system also taught the special dribble fast-break teams use most effectively. The coach must first demonstrate this dribble (or have someone demonstrate it for him).

This dribble, used consistently for the first time by the pros this year, is a high dribble—the ball bounces almost to the dribbler's neck and the dribbler "shoves the ball on" as it passes his hand, on the way down by "patting the side" of the ball, putting a slight back spin on it. The dribble looks somewhat slow, while the feet literally dance. This high dribble while moving fast enables the player to look over the court as he moves, keeping his head high because the ball, for the most part, is in the space between his head and his waist. The ballhandler can easily change directions, pass the ball or shoot from this dribble. He's perfectly balanced. He is doing all this while using a sprinting stride. From this move, strangely enough, the player is able to use a two-handed snap pass to his breaking teammates. This pass is often bounced off the floor for the cutter to run into. Try it—you'll like it.

12

Putting the Patterned
Fast Break Together

Many high school and even college coaches we've known, started out with little or no previous experience in the sport. Many didn't even play basketball in college or high school. Some starred in football, began coaching as a high school football assistant, with basketball coaching as an added duty. They were so successful at basketball, and liked it so well, that they quit football for full-time basketball coaching.

Sometimes those people make the best coaches. If they do, however, they have certain innate abilities, including that of choosing players to fit their style of play. Perhaps the most important ability a basketball coach should have is, of course, the ability to work with young people, to get the most out of them. He should be able to pick the "winners" from the "losers." He should be able to tell the difference between a "practice player" and a game performer. We've seen punters in football, for instance, who could kick the ball a mile in practice. Put them in game situations, in front of the crowds, and they sometimes kick the ball straight up. Contrast this, if you will, with the seemingly "poor" punter a coach often has to call on in emergencies. He seems to get his "best" boots off in those key moments.

Those "winners" are the players you want for your team. A good coach picks them instinctively. For the patterned fast-break system he not only has to pick the "winner," he also has to pick the special kind of winner who is fast enough and willing enough to stay up with the fast-break brand of ball. We've had some good, hard-working players who just couldn't stay up with our system. Some years we've actually been unable to unearth even five players who could play the fast-break game. For those years we had to change our style a bit, fit the players into a special system designed to fit their abilities. We never at any time, however, gave up the idea of the fast-break attack completely. We merely looked at our players, compensated for their lack of natural abilities, and let them do only what they could do well.

Thinking Ahead

A good coach looks for his players three or four years ahead of time. He plans his team for the coming year, plans the one for next year and looks for his future stars among the freshmen. He selects the "keys" to his attack, then designs the moves off his patterns to fit them. His keys, of course, are the players he will use to build around. He then supplements their abilities with the best players available to him to fit his team's needs for rebound power, defense, overall speed, outside shooting ability, inside scoring power and smartness of understanding of basketball problems. Sometimes, of course, players do not develop as expected; sometimes players move away and others move in. Adjustments must be made when these things happen, but the coach must never be caught without a definite plan in mind for several years to come. He cannot keep good teams coming along unless he has those plans. These plans fill the same needs in high school as recruiting in college. The high school coach doesn't have to recruit, but he does have to locate his future material, keep it coming along at a proper pace, and have it ready when he needs it.

Feeder Programs

"Feeder" programs in junior high schools aren't enough in themselves. Many junior high coaches like a different type of ball from the fast-break brand we prefer. They don't know what the fast-break coaches are trying to do with their players and the fast-break coaches don't know what the "slower brand" advocates are attempting with theirs. They may be successful with the slower brand of ball, so they play it in order to win. The players they use may not be the type of player the high school coach wants. There may not be one player on their junior high varsities coming up to senior high who will fit into the fast-break system.

We do not suggest that the junior high coaches be forced to use the senior high system. A coach is a proud person. He may give lip service to coaching like another coach, but he likes to go out and use his own style. If you force a coach to use your style, he'll quit and take another position as soon as he is able. If you want to keep a good man in junior high, then leave him alone, praise him, pay him well and hope that you can keep him a while. Don't worry about little things like systems. Organize your own. Scout out the players you want and keep your eyes on them. That's "system" enough!

The most elaborately planned feeder systems are often good only on paper. A good coach makes his own system. In fact, *he is the system*! He makes a town enthusiastic about basketball. We've found that any town is a good basketball town, providing the high schoool team is winning. Let them win over good teams for several years and everybody in town will attend the games against good competition. Real basketball fans won't come to see you win over a "setup." They aren't supposed to and you wouldn't want them to.

The best "feeder" system we ever had was an organization of three coaches who fed us about six good basketball players a year. Those players were good enough to win consistently. Most of those players went off to college, but most of them paid their own way. They didn't need college scholarships.

Sending Players on to College

We never felt that it was our purpose in coaching high school basketball to feed players into college teams. We like to see our players graduate and play in college if they want to, or need to, but we have never been part of a college feeder system and don't intend to become a part. If we can help our players after they graduate, we will do so, but we don't like college coaches calling us all the time, acting as if it were our duty to be an agent for them, urging our players to attend their colleges. High school athletics are ends unto themselves. High school basketball is a fun game.

College recruiting is a big business. We place loyalty to our own school and to our athletic program above that of being of service to colleges. We do not visit colleges for the purpose of bringing recruits to them. We do not "free load" at college games. Thus we owe nobody anything.

If a coach asks about one of our players, we tell him frankly and truthfully what we think our player can do for him in college. We also tell our players exactly what the situation is at the college in question. We tell him to look at the college coach and see if he would like to play under him for four years. We tell him to visit the college and see if he thinks he would like to live there four years; to see if the college teaches what he wishes to learn. We tell him to look at the team schedule he will probably play. Then we let him make his own decision. If he makes the right one, he can thank himself. If he makes the wrong one, he has only himself to blame.

Coaching the Fast Break Is a 12-Month-a-Year Business

No sooner is one season over than the coach must begin planning for the coming season. He makes his schedule, makes out his budget, gets his orders for new equipment into the sporting goods houses, then sets down and makes a formal estimate of the abilities of his players.

He selects his key men—his ballhanders, his rebounders

his pivot men and his corner men. He selects them, of course, for their speed of movement on the full court as well as their "position" ability. He writes down their abilities and he lists the things they need to work on. He writes a letter to each player pointing out those abilities, those weaknesses, and makes recommendations for their improvement. Then he calls each player in, has a heart-to-heart talk with him, explaining what he must do to make the team next year. He gives him a frank appraisal of what his abilities are and of his chances to make the first five. There should be no doubt left in the mind of the player as to just what he has to do to make the team. There should also be an understanding of what his closest rivals can do and what he must do to overcome a rival's advantage. The coach must be truthful with his players, offer no easy positions, yet he must not be so negative in his viewpoint as to discourage a possible starter.

Then he gives the player the letter he has prepared listing the things he must improve on and he tells him how to make those improvements. Next, he must make the gym available for the players to work out each week. We keep our gym open all summer, but we also have a special night when the players can get together. We are careful to see, however, that they break no rules against off-season practice. During the remainder of the school year we suggest that they come to the gym after school and work out on their own. Sometimes we open the gym for one night a week so the players can get together.

They'll come one night, but they won't come much more than that. We've found they'll often meet their friends at the YMCA or some goal on a side street or in a back yard for impromtu games. This is actually the best training they can get, working free-lance against friends with no supervision. When school closes for the summer, we still keep our gym open in the evenings. Players love to come down after work and shoot a few baskets. We've found they'll come if they know the gym will be open. We guarantee that and leave a ball out in the middle of the floor just for their use. Often we don't even hang around the gym ourselves. We once left a ball in the middle of the gym for three years. Nobody ever stole it. It disappeared one time, and we told the boys somebody had taken their ball so for them to find it—the ball came back the next day, and stayed there for the rest of the summer and up into football season. Often players would walk into the open doors of the gym, kick their shoes off, have a little game and then go on about their business. In the three years the ball was available, our teams won two state championships and played in the semi-finals the other year!

We invite college and professional players to come in and participate with our players during the summer months. We don't care too much about clinics and college coaches talking. We've found our players much prefer to play against and with the stars. They learn more by participation.

We like for our players to attend basketball camps, but more than anything else for *participation*. We tell them to watch the college athletes and to copy their moves. We aren't really excited about "name" college coaches; they really aren't very good as teachers. They admit themselves that their success depends mainly on recruiting.

We hit the height of our summer program along about the first of August. Summer camps in our area are full of good athletes at that time. Their instructors are often big names in the basketball world, so we make good use of them. We bring them to our players on familiar grounds. That way, *all* our players get the benefits, not just the ones who can afford to go off to a basketball camp. That's often too expensive for us.

Once we selected twenty-nine players for a camp, and got our fans to pay for them. That aroused a lot of interest in our team, but it also created quite a bit of dissention when only a few of those players made the team when they were seniors. Attending summer camp is no guarantee of success. We failed to explain that to fans and parents with special interest. In fact, there is no explaination you can give to a fond parent of a boy who fails to make the team as a senior. Parents rarely admit the boy just can't make it. They are prone to blame someone; the coach is available and usually gets the blame. There is little he can do about it.

Bringing the players to where our players are is our answer. We're often able to talk athletes into coming and participating with us just for the love of the game; they're willing to play just because they like to play. Of recent years, however, professional athletes expect pay for their time. If we need them, our fans provide that pay for us through donations.

Sometimes we schedule a series of summertime games, but we have to be careful not to break any rules. Many colleges do not allow their players to participate in summer contests. The pros have no summer rules, however, and our players can participate, providing not more than two of our varsity members play on the same team. Sometimes we schedule several games in an evening so they can all participate. We've found that "pick up" games are really better for our purpose and the players enjoy them more. We play "freeze out." Five players will start the evening, and continue to play against all challengers until they are defeated. The winner then stays up until they are defeated. That way we get game situations and it takes good teams to stay up all evening. It gives our players a lot of confidence when they defeat big name players. In all these summer games we must be sure to see the players don't fall into a slow brand of ball. Often college athletes, being a bit out of shape, suggest that everybody "slow it down."

We do not allow our players to do this. They are instructed to "come off the boards running" at all times. We put a summertime rule in that allows a player to walk off the court at any time and allow a substitute to walk in for him. These games are "gentlemen games." We play without a referee. If we are fortunate enough to have one, often some player will get mad at him, so we play simple rules like "driver calls a foul, takes the ball out of bounds"; "tieups go to the team that had possession"; and "no foul out for five fouls". We don't have much trouble. Players know we run troublemakers out of the gym.

We care very little about "clinics" that emphasize "basics" of basketball. Our players are usually too far advanced to be interested in basics. They want to *play*. Last year a professional team sent two of their star players up to give us a clinic. They brought playground goals with them on a station wagon that had their professional name emblazoned on it. They did this free, for the publicity. We let them talk a bit, demonstrate a bit, then we put them to work on one of our teams. They had been "holding clinics" all week and said they were "a bit tired," but they became competitive once they realized they were against good competition. Before they knew what was happening, the opposing team had them down by the score of 5 - 30, and they lost their first freeze-out game. They rested and before the evening was over were playing as if their whole world depended on it.

We received letters from them later telling us that they enjoyed being with us more than anywhere they visited. That's the reason we believe in securing the best talent available, putting it to use in the best way possible—that is, *playing* against and with our players. Lecturing is fine, but there's really no substitute for actual participation. As an added benefit the pros often pass the word on to college coaches about our good high school prospects. The coaches take their advice even more than their regular recruiters and, in that way, we make proper connections.

Athletes on their own seek out the college and pro players in preference to the college coaches—even the most famous. Summer camps featuring name coaches are still popular, but if you ask the athletes, they prefer the players. They pick an athlete, follow him around, copy his motions on the court. You can't beat that for real teaching. For that reason we prefer the *players* for our player "clinics." For coaches clinics, of course, name coaches are preferred. We only mention this because often high school coaches planning clinics miss this point of view. They give big publicity to clinics, hire expensive coaches, then are sometimes disappointed by the results as shown in their players. "Working clinics" featuring athletes often get better results.

About the first of August we begin to take time off. We arrange things so our players, even the most enthusiastic of them, are forced to take a break. We schedule nothing for them during the period of time the football team is getting ready for its season. We don't want them tired and stale before the basketball year begins.

Work in Guidance

With the start of school we check each athlete's schedule to be sure he has signed up for courses he is able to pass. Many athletes don't even know what some courses are all about. They line themselves up for difficult work they aren't qualified for and have little chance of passing. If somebody doesn't help them, they're likely to fail a course before they can be transferred to another class.

We do this through the school guidance office, but we can't really leave everything to them. They are highly overworked as it is and haven't time for special work with our athletes. However, we've always found them to be sympathetic and understanding.

We do not propose by this that a coach should try to sign his players up for "crip" courses under "easy" teachers. Many of our athletes are straight "A" students. In fact, we can easily remember at least three regulars who have been presidents of our student body and received honor academic scholarships to the state universities. However, there have been many boys we have rescued just in time because they unknowingly signed themselves up for courses like chemistry, advanced math or physics when they had been barely passing basic work.

There is no reason to allow them to work themselves into ineligibility. A little foresight here will save the coach a lot of trouble later. We've found that no teacher really wants to fail an athlete; however, the best teachers always have certain standards they won't lower for anyone. We wouldn't have it any other way. The coach can help his players find their own levels. However, like underscheduling games for a great team, he must not underschedule work for his athletes. The most important thing about a school is classroom work. Playing basketball is a game—a reward for work well done. School work comes first.

Fall Schedule

After school work is well underway, the basketball candidates usually come out with the cross country team for early season conditioning. They do not run the same schedule as the cross country team. They do conditioning exercises, road work like running hills, sprinting 30 yeards and walking 30 yards, running steps, doing pushups, working with the weights. If they choose to run with the cross country team, fine. Each player has a list of physical improvements he is expected to make. Other than that, he's on his own for the whole fall season. We open the gym each afternoon. If he wishes to do so after working outside, he may go into the gym, shoot a hundred or so long shots, work on hooks or drives or even simple dribble movements. Two or more players may team up if they wish, play two-on-two or three-on-three games at one basket. We do not allow team play at this time on the full court. These are the days we develop individual skills. Above all, however, we want our players to get into the best of condition. The football players who also play basketball are getting into good shape. We want our basketball players to keep up with them so that, by the time the first regular practice is called in November, everybody will be fresh and in the best of condition. Their feet must be toughened. We want no blisters on the first day of practice.

Blisters

Incidentally, if we discover a player who is prone to blister, we tape his feet up *before* he gets the blisters. We run a wide piece of tape around his foot just over the thick part where the blister usually rises; we put another wide piece of tape over his heel and another behind it.

We do not allow him to pull the tape off. If it comes off in the shower, we let it and tape him again the next day. After a week or so we allow the player to tape his own feet; but for those with weak ankles, we do the taping ourself. A player gets used to one person's tape jobs, so we don't switch around. We're with them all the time during the year, so we are the logical ones for that duty.

Beginning Regular Practice

When the first day of practice arrives, we start immediately at top speed. We waste no days getting ready. Our varsity players have all had experience running our patterns. The junior varsity players who have moved up were carried with us for several games during the past season. We moved them up for a game or so to travel with us, with the next year in mind. They ran our plays and drills on the junior varsity; but just to be sure there was no mistake, we brought them up, and had them run with the varsity so they would know exactly how we expected them to operate. We wanted them to get used to us personally and we wanted them to know we were counting on them—that junior varsity ball is only a preliminary to action on the varsity.

For the first two weeks our practices consist of drills. We hold no scrimmages. We run through our warm-ups first, then we make our drills competitive. Within two weeks time, we have our players begging for regular game scrimmages. By that time, we have developed our combination, have selected the five players who complement each other best as a team, and we're ready to go. We've sharpened our shooting eyes and we can go without dogging it on defense.

In the third week we begin scrimmaging in earnest. Everything after the warm-up period is "game situation." We use five players together at all times. On Tuesday and Friday we bring in regular officials, get out the clock controls, line up our score keepers, timers, and our statistic keepers, and run through regular game scrimmages. We assign our managers their game duties so that we run into no last-minute problems. We even bring in the record player and play music before these practice games in order to get the players used to the sounds of a regular contest. We appoint warm-up responsibilities to the team leaders; even have them run through their warm-ups without instructions from us, just as they will do in all regular games. With nobody timing them, they sometimes run the same drill too long and waste time. We want certain players to watch this.

Then we go over on the bench and watch the scrimmage exactly as we will do in regular games. The only reason we hold our scrimmages this way is that state rules do not allow us to hold scrimmages with other schools. Practice games are not allowed, so we make our Tuesday and Friday practices "game conditions." We do the same things on the last week before the first game. Then we figure we are ready.

The last week before the start of the season we call a Saturday morning practice. We do this for psychological reasons. We want a big build-up in the minds of the players. We want them to realize the importance of beginning the season properly and we want to go over any last-minute problems that might have arisen.

On that day we give them instructions for traveling. We give our talk about players representing our schools and acting as ambassadors, not as individuals. We list their responsibilities and we instruct them that they will always wear coats and ties on game days. We want them to be proud of themselves and proud of the school they represent. Once we made them wear look-alike blazers and ties in school colors. We don't do that anymore. We tell them to dress up in the latest fashion. We ask them to be "slick chicks", "classy dressers", the slicker the better. Then we check our players to find the ones who can't afford new clothes; we go out and raise some money to outfit them. They never know who gives the clothes to them; they just go up to a clothing store one day when we tell them to and the tailor outfits them. It's as easy as that. Businessmen of our city are glad to lend a helping hand and nobody is the wiser.

December Schedule

Our early season games are usually played on the road and with non-conference competition. We use these games for experimental purposes, to find our best combination.

Since our system of play depends mainly on speed and maneuverability, we substitute our guards in pairs to find the ones who work the best together. We are looking first for pass work; sheer speed on the straight-away is of next consideration. By this time we know the natural abilities of the players, but we are now looking for the ones who react the fastest and most naturally, under game conditions. Some react well in practice but just can't seem to make it in front of an audience. We weed those players out. We have an assistant coach sitting beside us looking for efficiency of movement in the big men under the boards while we are watching the speedsters. By the Christmas holidays we will have conferred, put our ideas together, selected our final starting five and begun to improve their basic movements. It isn't prudent at this time to try to change any individual movements radically. We wish only to refine them.

Work over the Christmas Holidays

After our last game in December, we dismiss until two days after Christmas. Then we begin our season all over again, but this time with the idea in mind of building our team up to reach its peak just in time for the post-season tournaments. We rate ourselves rather slowly and steadily; we do not attempt to "key our players up" for any special game. We build up the edge, keep it sharp, but we don't want to reach our peak too early and go stale for the tournaments. We want our players eager for the games; so during January and February we don't do much practice scrimmaging. We run our speed drills and reserve the real thing for our games only. Again, the thing we are emphasizing is getting players down the court and getting the ball to them.

When all this is done we are ready to enter basketball's "second season," the all-important tournaments. That's where the cheese is binding.

When we think of the total picture of what we are trying to accomplish, we can best illustrate it by pointing to the brand of ball played effectively by the NBA and the best college teams of the NCAA in 1970. Four teams are good examples of the patterned fast-break style we teach to our teams: the New York Knickerbockers and the Atlanta Hawks in the pros, and UCLA and Kentucky in college circles.

Pro basketball has changed its style in the last few years. It is now a "run and gun" game, with the best teams playing a full-court pressing defense and a full-court offense. The key to the success in this game is the ability of all players to shoot *facing* the basket. The play progresses without pause; for half-court style adjustments, a slow pivot style player (who must get his back towards the basket before he begins his offense) is out of place here. He often gets in the way of the patterns. Wilt Chamberlain plays this offense rather well when he is played on the off side and not in the pivot. When he plays the post, he waits for a cut instead of immediately getting rid of the ball. The defense collapses off on him and he looks bad on the fumbles that result. Chamberlain could be more effective if he forgot pivot play or was used in a slowdown brand of ball with other tall men near the basket.

The greatest mistake we've seen pro coaches make this year is planning a modern fast-break team with only one or two ballhandlers, and then allowing them to become isolated. Every player on the team must handle the ball. No press can be effective against them if they do that. The Lakers lost their title because they got to depending on Jerry West's ability to bring the ball up court against a tough defense. He got the ball up court, but in the last game of the series he was so tired by his efforts, so worried by the pressing defense, so exasperated by having the ball stolen from him at one key moment, that he was unable to operate effectively on the offense. His scoring out-put was limited. The New York Knicks did a beautiful job on him. Many coaches have said, "Don't try to stop the stars, let them get their points. Stop the rest of the team and you'll win." The Knicks put the squeeze on the star and won by an easy margin.

The Atlanta Hawks should have been in the championship series. They played the best brand of basketball, next to the Knicks. They perhaps would have had a better chance to win the title than the Lakers since their players were younger and the scoring was better balanced. They, too, had a superstar, but they didn't depend on him as much as the Lakers depended on West. They, too, played the modern brand of ball where everybody runs and everybody plays offense facing the basket. An injury to a key player killed Atlanta's chances.

Two college teams that played a brand of fast-break ball in the 1970 season (somewhat similar to the patterned style we advocate) were Kentucky and UCLA. Both teams use players who shoot facing the basket. Both teams have front line men who move over the court, take those quick push and jump shots. Neither of them depend on one or two men to handle the ball; both used well-balanced ballhandling and well-balanced scoring to achieve their victories. Both teams run well against pressure defenses. Ordinary teams had to play control or keep-away ball to stay in the game with them. Any team that tried to run with them usually ended up on the short end of the score in a hurry. Both teams were popular with the fans and played to packed houses every time they made an appearance.

Patterned fast-break ball is basketball at its best!

13

Some Special Public Relations and Coaching Considerations

One of the most vital areas a coach has to work in is public relations. A good coach must plan his own public image and that of his ball team. He must be sort of a press agent for his team and inadvertently himself in the process. The prestige of basketball in the school and the community depends on his efforts, his energy and his enthusiasm. If he drags around "poor mouthing," nobody will think much of or care much about his sport. He'll go on year after year explaining his defeats, and the lack of student or fan interest, on everything but the real thing—his own lack of ability. And nobody could care less because, by watching his teams, they do not know what a thrilling sport basketball can really be.

In those towns where such coaches operate, townspeople are often heard to remark that the place "has never been a basketball town." They prefer football or perhaps baseball.

Applesauce! Any town is a basketball town, providing it has a good basketball coach and he is not interfered with.

It is a good basketball coach's duty to promote basketball. He was hired for that purpose. No athlete will care much about the round ball sport in a "football town" or "baseball town" unless equal emphasis is put on basketball. A good hardwood coach does just that. He understands the big fact of sports life: that a town wouldn't be a football town unless the football team had a long record of winning football games! Hard-working football coaches gave the town the football name through long hours of planning and long hours of hard work, much of it physical. There's no room in the coaching fraternity for lazy people.

The basketball coach and the football coach don't really need to be jealous of each other. That often happens in schools where there is a lack of understanding between them and a lack of mutual respect. One sometimes attempts to belittle the other. Once upon a time the only "paying" sport in high school was football. It carried the load for all the other sports. That's changed a bit now that most towns have built big basketball arenas. Now huge crowds attend important basketball games and the sport adds to the school budget. Once upon a time the football coach was all-important because winning games meant everything to the high school expense account. As a result of the financial importance of the sport, football coaches were given the added duties of "athletic director." Being fanatics as far as football was concerned, they often hired the rest of the coaches as football assistants. Then he assigned them coaching duties in other sports including basketball, which at that time paid almost no revenue to the school. Just after World War II the great change began. Pro basketball became a popular sport and big arenas were built. New high school gyms were constructed, seating thousands of fans. Basketball became a money sport and coaches specializing in basketball were hired. For several years, however, they were still under the control of the football coach-athletic director who was often an "old timer" who couldn't care less about anything but football.

With the flood of new money into athletics in recent years,

the school athletic directorship has become a full-time position and basketball coaching has assumed a new status. The sport is not, however, equal to football in crowd appeal as a great outdoor spectacle. It probably never will, since it's an indoor sport. Playing during the winter months, as such, has certain limits placed on it.

Now that the basketball coach has been freed of his bondage to football controls, there's really no reason for basketball coaches to be jealous of football coaches or vice versa. The two sports actually complement each other. Fan interests, built up during the fall months on the gridiron, naturally gravitate in cold weather to the gymnasium. Coaches, understanding the problems of dealing with athletes, should actually become admirers of other coaches who are successful in dealing with those problems. A successful football coach should become a booster of a basketball coach equally successful, and a basketball coach a football booster. There's no longer any excuse for jealousy. There's real reason for professional loyalty.

We've heard high school coaches whine that nobody plays basketball in their town. That's a poor excuse for poor leadership. We know. We've taken on the task of building basketball in four different towns. All of those towns were known as losers; one hadn't won a basketball game in four years.

It takes about three years to convert a non-playing town into one that loves basketball. You have to step on some toes to do it, but the toes you have to step on actually only respect you the more for it when it becomes apparent you're a man with a motive. You can have yourself a winner anywhere, given a reasonable schedule and average talent. You can build that schedule and that talent yourself in any situation, but you have to use all the "tricks" and "gimmicks" to do it, though. Following are some of the gimmicks we have used successfully. We call them "the trappings of the great team."

Brochures

We publish our annual information sheet on basketball in the same way that colleges, summer camps and clinics do—in

the form of brochures. We always have these printed commer-
cially. We want everybody to know we're professional all the
way. Pamphlets mimeographed on school machines are often
less expensive, but we want more than that. We want first-class
publicity; mimeographed sheets are penny-ante, two-bit stuff,
more suitable for school classroom work. Kids know that. We're
building champions and that takes confidence. It costs only a
few cents more to go first class.

And as for expenses, we've often found some athlete's
father is ready and willing to pay the freight. If we accept his aid,
however, we make certain his son has already made his position
on the team. Then we'll accept his assistance. We wish no bribes
in exchange for a first-string position; we won't put ourselves
under obligation to any man. It's better to pay for the project
personally than to do that. We've never yet had to foot the bill,
however. Brochures are necessary expense account items.

Our brochure lists our complete squad, including those
expected to play on the junior varsity. We don't list the squads
separately; it's subtle psychology to make both a part of the
same grouping. We want no rivalry between the varsity and the
junior varsity. We list the squad, complete with height, weight
and class. We describe each player individually, tell of the talents
of each. We give a resume of the schedule and tell what the fans
can expect of our squad. We praise our squad, but we don't
over-praise—we tell our fans the truth. If you do that, after a
short while they'll begin to believe you and respect your
opinions—but only if you never try to fool them. We list our
schedule and we try in some way to promote the prestige of our
town in the bulletin by connecting our school with our "total"
community.

Our brochures are first distributed to our student body. We
direct all our publicity toward our students first. They are our
main body of support. The fans of the town are of secondary
consideration. They'll usually follow where the students lead.
We excite their interest with brochures and publicity, but we
know they won't attend too much unless the team is winning.
(We expect that of them—our whole nation is based on competi-

tion.) Champions attract the crowds—we aren't disappointed when they don't follow losing teams. We wouldn't have it any other way—"To the victor belong the spoils." That's human nature, else what would be the incentives of winning!

Score Cards

We have these available at the door of the gymnasium. They're printed with the home roster on the, with spaces left for visitors. The schedule is included as good publicity. We explain to the new fans how to use them in our "round ball preview" and we mention during our first games that they are available and that its more fun to watch a game and keep the individual statistics. You then have the inside dope on who is doing the scoring. Score cards also keep fans busy during the game, divert their attention, which makes for good sportsmanship.

We make our score card rather small, however, and print it on stiff paper. Fans don't usually carry something to write on with them. They need the stiffness, and the small size fits easily into pockets.

Sports Annuals

For a couple of years we experimented with sports "annuals" that consolidated all advertisements in one big brochure. We included all sports, major and minor in one issue.

It was our belief that businessmen didn't want to be bothered too much, that they considered such advertising merely as donations. We soon found out that the newness of sports annuals actually wore off even before football season was over. During basketball season fans wouldn't buy them and, by spring, you couldn't give them away. This happened in spite of the fact that we planned the program with all sports in mind. We left one area for basketball—printed pictures, a score card and historical information. We even had a wrestling score card printed in it.

It didn't work out very successfully. Now we plan our advertising methods in a much more up-to-date fashion. We visit all our advertisers each year, tell them our campaign for advertising. We explain that we intend to put out individual brochures in each sport and we brief them on our newspaper, TV and radio advertising. We use all those media on a paying basis. We expect them to publicize our ball teams free, but we've found that the news medium has changed. They don't hire many reporters any more to get out and interview players and coaches. As a result of the death of the old-fashioned reporter, we expect the obvious—news media report the results of the games and have little space for advance information, so we buy ourselves that advance advertising. We use the same source of revenue as the news media corporate advertising. In fact, we often beat them to the punch. We get to the source before the news media salesmen. Once upon a time we sent out news releases. College and pro teams do the same thing, but today even those aren't used. It's easier for overworked sports editors to pick their news pre-digested off the wires, so we bow to the inevitable, buy our own publicity, work up our own layouts, and see that it gets in on the proper day.

We visit our prospective advertisers in the summer months, tell them frankly of our plans and ideas, and offer them their choice of advertisement—on the radio, TV, in the newspapers or in our program. We tell them our plans early enough so they have funds left in their corporate budgets. Often we find they like our ideas. We advertise our product and they advertise their own with us, with the "soft sell" idea of their product mentioned incidentally with us. We have to be careful here, however. If we benefit as individuals from such advertising, we could be ruled professional; there's little real difference in this kind of advertising and football program advertising.

Last year, just before our first basketball game, we put full page spreads in the Sunday newspaper. We used only "wholesome" products. We published an amusing picture of our squad drinking a local favorite bottled drink. The picture was entitled "get that barefoot feeling," and it showed our squad relaxing with the drink, their big feet very obvious. Fans smiled when they saw it and they became "indulgent" toward us. That's the attitude we wish to create. The advertisement drew state-wide interest. We were very careful to have our schedule and roster of players in the most obvious positions. Unless our own product is the chief thing we are selling, we wouldn't agree to such an arrangement.

We intend to do the same thing even with our sports program next year. We've been printing full pages of advertising in our program with nothing else on the page. We do not intend to do that any more. We've found that our printer is now getting the most of our money. We intend to put a stop to that by printing the advertising and the information on the same pages. The advertising will be smaller, the information more complete, and it will cost us less in the long run. We'll keep most of our advertising dollars instead of paying them out for expenses.

We do not intend to put out a basketball program this year. It is our plan to print a brochure at the beginning of the season which will be much smaller than an ordinary program, almost in book form. Then for each game we'll print a score card that has information (gathered in the pre-season) on every team we meet. The center of this sheet will be the score card part. We intend to print only one gatefold page on post card type paper. The information on visiting teams will be on the back of the fold along with the advertising. Anything else of interest we wish to print will be along the borders of the face of the score card. This will be about the size of a file folder and on the same type of paper. We believe these cards will be the most pleasing to everybody of any style we have yet uncovered.

Annual Team Nickname or Sports Mascot

We have also advertised a bit in conjunction with automobile dealers. For example—we usually adopt "annual" nicknames for our ball team, and place those names or emblems on our uniforms for one year only. Usually the name we pick is somewhat humorous ("tickles the fan's innards") that gets the fan chuckling a bit when he thinks of us, yet respecting us for our basketball ability.

A few years ago we traveled far and wide over the state, so we adopted the nickname "Road Runners." We put a full page advertisement in the paper in conjunction with the local Plymouth dealer. It showed our high school team gathered around a "Roadrunner" sports car. The advertisement was basically built around our team and our schedule. Fans liked it and the picture made the Chrysler Corporation Trade magazine. There were no real "ethics" involved in this. A high school team's name has little real advertising value to a corporation and all we got out of it was the advertisement. We allow anyone to advertise in our ordinary programs. We see no objection to it. In fact, we allow any corporation to do the same thing. All we want is the advertising.

We adopt our annual nicknames for another reason. We believe it helps give color to sports reporting. Nicknames used annually year after year, however, can sometimes become very boring. For instance, reporters are sometimes hard put to think up something new, so they annually write "Today the *'Green Wave' washed* into town" or "It was a dark evening for the locals as the *'Purple Tornado' blew* their once-great record right out of the stadium."

The "Road Runner" title we adopted one year even had fans writing little ditties about it. Opposing fans were "hanging" the roadrunner in posters and our fans were coming back with "Look at that roadrunner's eyes. He's playing 'possum. You can't catch a Roadrunner." The "Beep-Beep" call was very popular.

The next year we adopted the nick name "The Wild Bunch" since they played that way. They were a colorful crew that excited sports writers. Sometimes they were world beaters— sometimes they barely squeaked through. Fans liked the name, wore cowboy hats, and carried cap pistols. Even sportsmen who don't attend games follow our publicity antics, enjoy reading about them, and wonder what we'll do next.

We don't know either, right now. The secret of the success of nicknames lies not in selecting them before the season, but in allowing the teams to develop their own personality (sort of name themselves). Then when one becomes appropriate, we adopt it. This isn't a truly artificial creation. It happens naturally.

We also try to make our press releases colorful and unusual. We were especially successful not so long ago when we were reporting a baseball game. Activity ended in the tenth inning with the teams deadlocked 6 to 6. It became too dark to see the ball. After we got through reporting statistics, the reporter asked us why we quit. We answered, tongue in cheek, "It was milkin' time." That was the heading of the article the next morning: "*Teams play until milkin' time.*" Of course, most of the boys involved never saw a cow, but the wires picked it up. An ex-ballplayer sent us a copy of the same writeup in a New Orleans paper; a week later a GI from town wrote us from San Diego enclosing the same little clipping about playing until milking time. One colorful word made the difference.

Player Nicknames

We believe also that a ball team creates a "positive" attitude or a "negative" attitude among fans the moment it trots on the hardwood. We try to get the fans on our side immediately, at their first impression. We don't want them to think we are clowns, however. We wish them to respect us. We wish them to adopt us. One way we do this is to have our nicknames emblazoned on the back of our warm-ups. It helps fans to get acquainted with our players by being able to call them by their nicknames. We allow our players to pick their own names— usually they already have them—"Monk," "Stack," "Lyrch," "Go-Go," "Lo-Lo," "Baby Lou," "Happy," "Bo-Bo," "Stork," "Whopper." We even had one tiny guard called "The Jolly Green Giant." One called himself "The King."

Fans, on seeing these names, immediately begin to associate themselves with one or another player, and sometimes start up a conversation. That gets folks on our side.

How to Get the Student Body Interested

We don't have much trouble interesting the boys in bas- ketball. We just concentrate our attentions on the girls to get them interested and attending the games. The boys then follow their leadership.

We have special "assemblies" just for girls. We introduce the players, demonstrate the plays, show what we are trying to do, explain what each athlete is especially good at, and form "pep" clubs out of the girls so they will feel a part of it.

We have that pep club on the stage at rallies. Most of them are volatile and loud, and they make the best fans to pep things up. We also often add boys who are "trouble makers" around school to this pep group. They thus find something to center their activities on.

We don't especially care about having the school band at our rallies. We prefer peppy combos. They play the music we like, often modify and modernize the "'Star Spangled Banner" of basketball—"Sweet Georgia Brown." Students react to this and our students figure "we're the latest."

When we put on our "student clinics," we gear them to the students' level, and include the things they like. We select their combos. We clown a lot, a-la-Globetrotters. We can actually do everything the 'Trotters do, so we enjoy ourselves in a completely "planned" clinic that wastes no time, keeps the fans laughing or smiling and moves along efficiently. We try to make the clinics truly professional entertainments. We even have our athletes who play musical instruments or sing, perform for the students.

We have never had any comments on our "shows," except those of approval. When fans come to see us once, we expect them to come back again, and our best fans are our own student body. We concentrate on them. Their fathers, mothers, uncles and aunts follow—even the neighbors.

Cheerleaders

Our cheerleaders are always considered "part of the act." They travel along with us wherever we go. We use them as the supporting cast of our stars, the players. Ours are dancing, singing cheerleaders, using rhythmic chants and yells that make of our gym a "community sing." The fans "cut loose," enjoy themselves and feel an integral part of the show. Most of them wouldn't miss a game. We like this new "fan participation." It's sometimes better than the game itself and it isn't directed at the rivals across the court. In fact, it isn't directed at anybody. It's merely a social gathering, with the cheering for the team as an added attraction.

Get Luck on Your Side

This is often merely a pose, but it's usually good for the players to be able to smile a little at frivolous things. Players are not actually superstitious, and neither are the coaches; but they like to blame a lot of things on "luck," the "wheel of fortune" and just plain chance. Every coach likes to have the odds on his side, so he often "plays around with" superstitions. He enjoys wearing the same coat or tie, the same tie clasp or loud-colored socks and vest. He carries four leaf clovers or horse shoes. Those objects often become trademarks—coaches are identified with them and fans look for them before the game as "added security." Actually they are little more than conversation pieces that go with the extraordinarily good teams. They are the "trappings" of the game. Fans indulgently join in the fun.

We often suggest that our players and fans work to get good luck on our side. We've had ladies tell us they are wearing their "good luck" dresses. We've had players to protest against getting uniforms cleaned for fear of losing our luck. We often abide by their wishes. Team morale is a strange and often fragile thing. We have no desire to play around with it. We have our desk loaded with good luck charms that fans have sent to us. We keep our shoes full of four leaf clovers.

Once somebody sent us a figure of a little Indian rain god—not more than one day later we received an unexpected blow from out of the blue. Through no fault of ours, we were forced to forfeit all our games for the year. I went home, took that fat little figure out back of my house and offered it as a sacrifice to the lake nearby!

We're not really superstitious, but if a black cat crosses our path before a game, we turn around, take another path to the gym. We don't want to take any chances.

Remember Who the Boss Is

Have fun, but keep the clip board and the whistle between you and the players. We've never lost a star, but we've never petted one either. Every player works out just like the rest. No player is allowed special privileges. We set certain punishments for certain offenses, but we never make them so difficult that we lose a player because of minor problems.

We tell the boys not to smoke, drink or stay out late at night with the "wild, wild women." If we catch them, we punish them—within reason. We never pay any attention to what "someone tells us" about the players and we don't go spying on the boys or calling them up at night to see if they are at home. If any player appears to be out of shape, we have a little talk with him and tell him his tongue is showing. And we don't worry too much about girl friends. It's natural that players should be interested in girls and that they be interested in players; however, we warn them that if they become so tied down with a girl friend that they become just an escort, then they'd better give up trying to be an athlete.

Once we gave an ultimatum to our squad; told them they'd have to give up girls or give up ball. After the meeting our star player came up to us, told us "You want me to tell you now, Coach?" I thought fast, and told him I'd let him know when the decision was to be made. He's probably still waiting for me to tell him when. Since then we've never put ourselves in a corner where we couldn't back out.

Aid to the Players

We believe in getting close to our players, but we let them alone except where basketball is concerned. We help them with transportation problems, we see that they have proper clothes to wear, we help them make decisions on where to go to college, but mainly we give advice only when asked. The young people make their own decisions in the long run. We let it be known from the first day that, on the basketball court, it's a man's ability that gets him his place (plus the way he fits into "the combination"). We tell him to be sure to look to see if the team keeps scoring efficiently when he is playing. That's the real secret to whether he's going to play or not—it really has nothing to do with "how many points" he scores personally. Anybody can hang around and get a basket or so.

We assure them that all players will receive a square deal. No one can ask for more than that.

Coach and Player Working Together

We let our boys in on our every secret. We tell them before the season starts who will probably be all-state and why we intend to push them for post-season honors. We tell them who the best players are and why they are the best. We talk individual faults over with them, especially the "almost" players—the ones whose shots keep rimming the hoop and keep falling out. We talk to the "practice" starts who can't hit under game pressure and help them overcome their failings.

We talk about our problems and our opponents', including road trips with "homer" officials. We explain what we have to do to win—and that is what we intend to do.

When we plan to get the newspapers on our side by bragging or "poor mouthing," we tell the players what our object is. We don't want to fool him, too.

And above all, we explain to our players how we expect our combination to work, where we expect each player to shoot from and what we expect him to do on defense. When a player disagrees with us, we tell him frankly what we think and why. If he still continues to disagree, then we allow him to drop from the squad.

Bad Language

We never allow the use of foul language on one of our squads. We never allow card playing. We never allow arguments among players. We tell them frankly that if they can't get along, then we'll have to get rid of one of them. If a substitute is involved, we call him in and frankly tell him he is more expendible than the varsity member. If the varsity member is at fault, we call him in and correct him.

We never allow a player to "talk back" or argue with us over a correction. I can remember only one time that a player ever actually "cussed" us. That player never stepped on the court again, even though he was only a junior and his father was an old friend of mine. (Nobody ever pressured us about the dismissal.)

Penalties for Minor Offenses

We set minor penalties for loss of temper, double dribbles, failure to shoot when open, or failure to pass at the right moment. We make of them penalties that "amuse" the other players. For example—one year we had a player who slammed the ball against the floor on a missed shot or a walk. We set the rule that if anyone lost his temper at himself and showed it, he would have to run over and bite the mat on the wall behind the goal. Sometimes during the early season we stopped and watched as he walked slowly over and bit the mat. At times other players would double over, sometimes even roll on the floor laughing at the sulky star. It worked, though. He didn't do much biting after Christmas.

Horseplay in the Gym

We allow some of it. We think players should enjoy themselves. We don't hurry them through their showers; we let them stay until they're ready to go home.

However, we never allow horseplay on the gym floor. We're too busy before and during practices. After we're through we allow the players to practice fancy dunks or dribbles if they wish. Some become fantastically adept at it.

Music for Practice

We always have a record player in our gym for practices. We play Hammond organ music before formal drills begin and sometimes during the drills, stopping the music only for instructions. We pick our music carefully, however, for its soothing qualities. Often the athletes wish to bring loud "rock" music; we do not allow that. Off-beat records bounce from wall to wall in the gymnasium and sound like chaos!

The Coach on the Bench

I've heard it said that a coach should work all week in practice, then go home and let his team play—he'd win more games that way. And I once heard a football coach telling about a "coaching job" he did on one of his budding young kickers. "When he came to me," he said, "he could kick the ball fifty yards on the fly. When I got through with him, he was kicking the ball more than thirty-five."

Both of these stories tell of the dangers of "over coaching." The game of basketball is really a simple game of putting the ball through the hoop. A lot of "trappings" have grown up around the sport—scouting, studying films, making game plans, preparing special defenses and special offenses. All the trappings are sometimes enough to frighten the most seasoned campaigner— until he realizes that the game is still a simple game of doing what you have to do to win it. Fancy words may make it seem complicated, but it's still a game of five enthusiastic athletes playing against five others. The team that works hardest on defense usually wins, all other things being equal.

The coach should be, and is, the team's faculty adviser. The boys are supposed to do the playing—the coach is there to advise them, keep them enthusiastic. He should sit quietly on the bench and help them when they need help—point out a few little needed changes—take time out and advise them whenever they get a little shook up.

When they're doing well, he leaves them alone. That's the way it should be. He has no business putting on a show before the crowds, displaying bad manners and a bad temper. I've never seen a dishonest official. (I've seen a few lazy ones who needed to be told to get on the ball. And I sometimes offered that suggestion quietly during time outs and only when speaking to them face to face and in the way of constructive criticism.) I don't care for childish displays of temper. The coach has too much to do to worry about the officiating. He has to watch all five of his players on offense, note the ones who are forgetful of their patterns. I like to see players free lance during games, but only whenever necessary and, even then, more often toward the end of the game when the defense is tiring.

The coach has to watch his players on defense to see how they are switching and charging. He has an assistant beside him to watch the opposing team, look for the leading scorers, look for their weakness on defense and to offer suggestions as to the possible change of patterns.

If our system of play is working well enough for us to get good shots and rebound position, we rarely change, except where we might do somethingg if we are missing constantly. We rarely make much change in our regular pre-game plans. Too much change usually upsets our own team. With all these things to look after, we can't see how a coach has time to referee also—unless he isn't really a coach, but is, like Bob Cousey, Coach of the Cincy Royals, described himself—"A glorified baby sitter."

A coach has to be extra careful, when he gives instructions for a change, that all his players are listening to him. One player with thoughts that are far away can sometimes ruin the best laid plans.

We ask our assistant coaches sitting with us on the bench to never talk to our players at time out. Many times we call our players to the bench merely to rest them. They don't need instruction. Sometimes they merely need a confident look in the eyes by the coach and a smile of approval on his lips. We don't even like to call time outs too often early in the game. Often we can give instructions to our players by talking to them along the sideline or by calling one over before foul shots or during throw-ins. We don't even do that much.

We've learned over the years to sit quietly on the bench, let the stomach muscles tie up into giant knots, take a digestion tablet now and then, keep the team ahead of or close to their opposition until the last three minutes. Then, really play the game all out.

Sometimes a close game can be torn apart in the first two minutes after the half. Sometimes it happens in the first minutes of the fourth quarter. If it looks like the game is going right down to the wire, then the coach had better sit up and work for his money. Those few moments of great pressure are what he's paid for. If he cracks when the going gets tough; if he doesn't glory in the critical moves; if he doesn't come alive at those times, then he wasn't born to be a coach. He should love those great moments. That's what the game is all about. That's where the action is. Those fleeting seconds are worth all those off season months of work and waiting.

When the game is over, win, lose or draw, the coach meets with his rival and shakes his hand. Then tight lipped and poker faced he goes to his own dressing room, busies himself doing something to work off his pent-up emotions. If he loses the game, he keeps his mouth shut. If he wins, he remembers he might have been the loser and that there is always another day, so he's generous with his opposition. No one wants elaborate condolences, however, especially by the winner, but a little truthful praise never hurts. If the other side wins then there's no need to add to his praise. The victory alone is enough and there's no need to belittle your own players.

If they need talking to, then do it in private, not in front of the press. They never forget a dressing-down in public. It cowes them and it never helps them to be better players. It often builds resentment and that resentment sometimes bubbles over and the players actually begin to blame their coach.

Last winter we once had a fine player from an opposing team come over before our game with their school and praise our record. When the play began we saw what was the matter, their team spirit had been broken. We had no trouble beating them. We spoke to their coach after the game, he immediately began to sing the praises of our players and started condemning his own. His team of great prospects never recovered, even for the tournament.

The best advice we can give to the coach on the bench is to keep his mouth shut and his eyes open. He might learn something.

Preparing for Tournaments

At this time the coach doesn't have to pep talk his boys. They'll be ready. But he does have to work them in a new manner. They're a bit tired of the same old warm-up drills, for instance. They could do with a bit of variety.

We don't believe, however, that the team should get completely away from basketball as a change-of-pace. One college coach we know trained his NCAA bound team by playing volley ball. Needlessly to say he was ridiculed when his team was swamped.

The coach should not change too many "habits" formed in the regular season, but some changes are necessary. Tournament teams are all good teams, so a more cautious brand of ball should be played. The opposition should be carefully studied and gone over with the squad. Care should be taken not to build the opposition up as supermen in the minds of the players. They should KNOW they CAN win.

The week end at the tournament in motels or hotels should be carefully planned. Frankly, we think the players should not be isolated from their schoolmates, but should be allowed to join in some of the fun. However, the squad should be housed so that when the time comes for them to rest, it will be easy to isolate them.

The players should work out briefly the morning before each game, if only to do a bit of shooting. Half court work is always sufficient. No full court running—just a little work on patterns and a bit of sharpening the eye for the basket.

The team should always be cautioned that it comes to the tournament to play three games. The last one is the most important. They should pace themselves; when any game is won the varsity players should be taken out and substitutes played the rest of the way.

During tournament play the coach usually doesn't have much trouble with the boys who are actually playing. This is true down through the first three or four substitutes, but athletes who haven't really done much all year but sit on the bench usually are restless, especially if they are seniors. It would be better to take ten of your seasoned players with you, pick as the other two the best players off the "B" team. They will be easy to handle. You can even use them to help manage. They're looking forward to next year.

Some Little Things That Made the Difference

Confidence is important. We once had a team that knew it could win. We didn't have to tell them, either. We always line a heavy schedule for our teams in the belief that the best competition gives the players confidence. After they've played the best teams in the state, they come back home and often swamp local competition. It has happened that way year after year. We have no reason now to disbelieve it. The team we fielded that year was seasoned and talented. They beat most of their local competition easily, even went to Florida, played the University Freshmen a good game. They had also met the University of North Carolina Freshmen along with Furman and Clemson Frosh.

They were fast and accurate. At the end of the season we made the playoffs, traveled to Durham and Duke University for the tournament.

We checked into our hotel and the players immediately disappeared, as usual, headed downtown to sightsee and do some shopping. They came back an hour later all wearing gold key chains. We inquired as to the reason, were told confidently, "Why we got these for the gold basketballs they're going to present us when we win the title." They won the title with not too much trouble. The margin of victory for the championship game was somewhere near 15 points. One big forward said to us, sort of apologetic, as the game ended, "Coach, we beat them too badly." We haven't often had material that good for our teams but we've seen a lot of good ones come and go. We've learned the hard way that often THE LITTLE THINGS make the difference in the great teams and the also-rans. Sometimes an attitude; sometimes it's only one player who is a bad actor that upon looking back at the year we realize we would have been better off to have dropped him when he was a sophomore and his bad traits became apparent. A team is only as good as its worst member. Drop the problems. You'll be better off in the long run.

We can at this moment remember at least four state titles that were lost because of little things. It's the story of the kingdom that was lost for want of a horse shoe nail, all over again.

One tourney we lost because a star player stepped on a stray basketball the last practice we held before the tournament, sprained his ankle. We've never allowed a stray ball around a court since then.

Another title was lost because with the score tied in the championship game, two minutes to go, a boy fumbled a tip on a fast break set up, recovered, then tried to pass the ball to the guard cutting after the guard was already past. He threw the ball a bit late, caused his teammate to walk. We lost possession, the opposition scored and we were also-ran.

We lost another championship because a player was prone to throw his forearm in close competition. He did that in a semi-final game, got tossed out and there went our chances.

A missed goal tending call cost us another. The officials missed it, but our players quit, turned and looked at the officials, seemingly wanting to argue. In the meanwhile the opposing team took the ball and scored. We never caught up. We were too busy thinking about the missed call. We were also-rans.

The most unexpected title we ever won was by a team that almost collapsed in mid-season. For some unknown reason this team with a poor record suddenly began to win in February, never lost another game, became a happy-go-lucky gang that rollicked along all the way to the title.

Two titles were lost because players stepped on boundary lines. Its been that close for many years. Another game we came so close to but didn't win we remember was lost because we, as the coach, couldn't figure a way to communicate with our players. With a minute and a half to go, behind one point, no time outs left and the ball in our possession, we sat there as a fine little player almost completely exhausted tried desperately to think what to do. He finally edged his way in one side (the other team let him), but he stepped on a line; they got the ball out of bounds and we were also-rans by one point.

We remember these things, but then we have the thought that all the other coaches can remember small things that caused them to wash out of the tournaments also.

That only goes to bear out the thought we wish to make here. That is: All other things being equal, IT'S THE LITTLE THINGS THAT COUNT. It's the little things falling your way that make the champions. It takes a lot of work to get that far, though—to the place where all things are equal. If and when you get there, my friend, we hope those little things fall your way. They have for us a goodly share of the time. We have no gripe coming.

Basketball has been good to us. We hope we've been good for it.

Index